Gooseberry Patch®

Fast-Fix MEALS

Gooseberry Patch
2545 Farmers Dr., #380
Columbus, OH 43235

www.gooseberrypatch.com
1•800•854•6673

Copyright 2008, Gooseberry Patch 978-1-62093-135-6
Fifth Printing, December, 2013

Do you have a tried & true recipe...

tip, craft or memory that you'd like to see featured in a **Gooseberry
Patch** cookbook? Visit our website at **www.gooseberrypatch.com**,
register and follow the easy steps to submit your favorite family recipe.
Or send them to us at:

Gooseberry Patch
Attn: Cookbook Dept.
2545 Farmers Dr., #380
Columbus, OH 43235

Don't forget to include the number of servings your recipe makes,
plus your name, address, phone number and email address.
If we select your recipe, your name will appear right along with
it...and you'll receive a **FREE** copy of the cookbook!

CONTENTS

SIZZLING *Skillets* 5

TOSS-TOGETHER *Suppers* .. 35

JUST *Pop* **IN THE** *Oven* 65

SIMMERING *Soup Pots* 95

DINNER ON A *Bun* 117

SPEEDY *Sides* 139

CRUSTY BREAD & A *Salad* ..167

Desserts **IN A JIFFY** 193

Dedication

For everyone who looks forward to a delicious home-cooked meal at the end of the day...dinner is served!

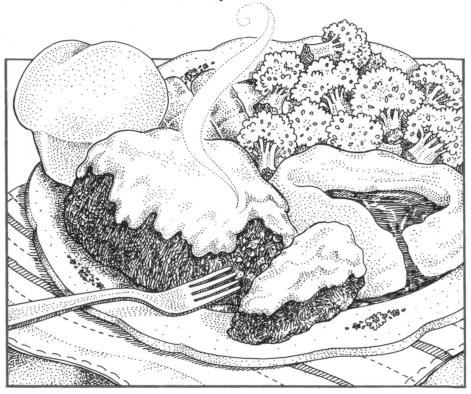

Appreciation

A sincere thanks to all our friends who shared your tastiest, speediest recipes with us!

SIZZLING
Skillets

Chicken Fajitas

Teresa Potter
Branson, MO

Our family loves Mexican food and this is one of our favorite ways to enjoy it. For a lighter meal, serve in bowls without the tortillas...delicious!

1 to 2 T. olive oil
4 to 6 boneless, skinless
   chicken breasts, thinly sliced
3 to 4 green peppers, sliced
2 red peppers, sliced
1 onion, sliced
1 to 2 T. chili powder

1/2 t. ground cumin
salt and pepper to taste
16-oz. can diced tomatoes
16-oz. can black beans, drained
   and rinsed
2 c. cooked brown rice
10 8-inch flour tortillas

Pour enough oil in a large skillet just to coat the bottom; heat over medium-high heat. Add chicken and cook just until no longer pink; add peppers, onion and seasonings. Stir-fry until chicken is golden and vegetables are tender. Add tomatoes with juice and beans. Cook until liquid is evaporated; add rice and stir together. Warm tortillas in microwave. Place heaping spoonfuls of chicken mixture onto each tortilla and fold ends over. Serves 4 to 6.

Starting a speedy supper? Check the recipe first, to make sure you have everything on hand before you begin...no last-minute trips to the store for a forgotten ingredient!

SIZZLING *Skillets*

Beef Skillet Fiesta

Kimberly Archer
Sumner, IL

My mom used to fix this all-in-one-pan meal often as I was growing up and we all loved it. Now sometimes I'll surprise Mom by making it and having her over for supper. We add a piece of buttered bread and enjoy the memories.

1 lb. ground beef
1 T. oil
1/4 c. onion, diced
14-1/2 oz. can whole tomatoes
12-oz. can corn
1-1/4 c. beef broth

1 t. chili powder
2 t. salt
1/4 t. pepper
1/4 c. green pepper, diced
1/4 c. red pepper, diced
1-1/3 c. instant rice, uncooked

In a large skillet over high heat, brown ground beef in oil, chopping into coarse chunks. Drain; add onion and turn heat down to medium. Cook until onion is tender, but not brown. Add undrained tomatoes, undrained corn, broth and seasonings; bring to a boil. Stir in peppers; return to boiling. Stir in rice; cover and remove from heat. Let stand for 5 minutes. Fluff with a fork and serve. Serves 6 to 8.

If your family loves spicy food, why not mix up your own chili powder blend? Fill a shaker with 2 teaspoons garlic powder, 2 teaspoons cumin and one teaspoon each of cayenne pepper, paprika and oregano. It's easy to adjust to your own taste.

Honey Chicken Stir-Fry

Lynn Ruble
Decatur, IN

Measure out the seasonings before you begin to stir-fry...
you'll find this dish goes together very quickly.

1 to 2 lbs. boneless, skinless
   chicken strips
4 T. honey, divided
1 egg, beaten
1/3 c. plus 1 T. water, divided
1 t. Worcestershire sauce
1/2 t. dried thyme
1/4 t. lemon-pepper seasoning
1/4 t. garlic powder

1/8 t. dried oregano
1/8 t. dried marjoram
2 T. oil
1 T. cornstarch
16-oz. pkg. frozen stir-fry
   vegetables
1/4 t. salt
cooked rice

Combine chicken, 2 tablespoons honey, egg, 1/3 cup water, sauce and herbs; set aside. Heat oil in a wok or large skillet over medium-high heat. Add chicken a few pieces at a time; cook and stir until golden. Remove chicken from wok; keep warm. Mix cornstarch with remaining honey and water; set aside. Add vegetables to wok; sprinkle with salt. Cook over medium heat until vegetables begin to thaw; drizzle with cornstarch mixture. Continue cooking until vegetables are tender; stir in chicken and heat through. Serve with rice. Serves 4 to 6.

Use a long-handled wooden spatula for stir-frying, to lift and turn the food easily without scratching the pan.

SIZZLING *Skillets*

Rustic Kielbasa Skillet

Pat Crandall
Rochester, NY

This is one of my husband's favorite quick-cook meals, so I make it often. A hearty country bread completes the meal.

12 new redskin potatoes, quartered
1 to 2 onions, quartered
1 green pepper, diced
1 T. olive oil

3/4 c. chicken broth
2 T. soy sauce
1-1/2 lbs. Kielbasa, sliced 1/2-inch thick

In a large skillet over medium heat, cook potatoes, onions and pepper in oil until potatoes are golden. Add broth and soy sauce; cook until potatoes and vegetables are fork-tender. Toss in Kielbasa and cook until heated through. Serves 3 to 4.

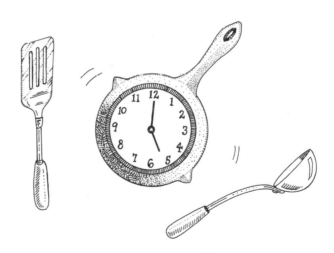

Smoked sausage is a great choice for fast-fix meals...just heat and serve. Different flavors like hickory-smoked or cheese-filled can really jazz up a recipe, or try smoked turkey sausage for a lean and healthy alternative.

Simple Tater Supper

Janie Reed
Gooseberry Patch

An old-fashioned favorite that's easy to prepare on short notice.

5 to 6 redskin potatoes, cubed
2 to 3 T. oil
12-oz. can spiced luncheon
   meat, cubed

4 eggs, beaten
8-oz. pkg. shredded Colby Jack
   cheese

Place potatoes and oil into a hot skillet over medium heat. Cook, turning often, until golden and nearly done through. Add meat; continue to cook and turn until potatoes are completely cooked. Whisk eggs together; pour over meat and potatoes. Lower heat and continue cooking, turning often, until eggs are cooked. Sprinkle cheese on top. Cover for 2 to 3 minutes, until cheese has melted. Serve immediately. Serves 4 to 5.

Let the rest of the family help! Younger children can tear lettuce for salad...older kids can measure, chop, stir a skillet and maybe even help with meal planning and shopping.

SIZZLING *Skillets*

Speedy Goulash

Laura Witham
Anchorage, AK

*I love goulash! After some experimenting, I came up with what
I believe is the easiest and tastiest recipe for goulash.*

1 lb. ground beef
1 onion
2 cloves garlic
1 T. Hungarian paprika
1/2 T. ground coriander
1/2 T. ground cumin

1/4 t. nutmeg
14-1/2 oz. can diced tomatoes
3 T. sour cream
salt and pepper to taste
8-oz. pkg. elbow macaroni,
   cooked

Brown ground beef in a large skillet over medium heat. While beef is
cooking, grate onion and garlic directly into beef; add spices and mix
well. When beef is just cooked, drain. Add tomatoes with juice; warm
through. Stir in sour cream, salt, pepper and cooked macaroni; serve
immediately. Serves 6.

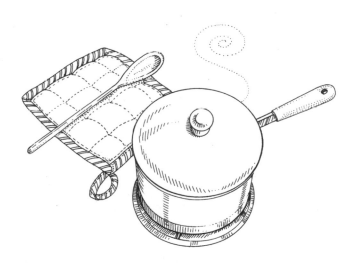

When pasta is on the menu, put a big pot of water on the stove
as soon as you get home. It'll be boiling in no time!

Shellye's Pizzadillas

Shellye McDaniel
DeKalb, TX

My kids love quesadillas and pepperoni, so I combined them for a creation that quickly became a favorite.

20 8-inch flour tortillas
3 c. shredded Colby Jack cheese
4-oz. pkg. sliced pepperoni

14-oz. jar marinara or pizza sauce, warmed

Heat an electric griddle to 375 degrees or heat a griddle pan over medium-high heat. For each quesadilla, lightly spray one side of a flour tortilla with non-stick vegetable spray; place on griddle sprayed-side down. Sprinkle with 1/4 cup shredded cheese; layer desired amount of pepperoni slices over cheese. Top with a second sprayed flour tortilla. Toast on both sides until golden. Remove from griddle and cut into wedges. Serve with marinara or pizza sauce. Makes 10 servings.

Non-stick vegetable spray is a great way to save both time and calories when fixing a stir-fried or sautéed recipe. Look for olive oil and butter spray for added flavor.

SIZZLING *Skillets*

Yummy Corn Quesadillas

Misty Bell
Denison, TX

Garnish with a dollop of guacamole or sour cream...or both!

2 yellow onions, sliced
4 T. olive oil, divided
8 to 12 6-inch corn tortillas
16-oz. pkg. shredded
   Monterey Jack cheese

3-lb. deli roast chicken,
   shredded or cubed

In a large skillet over medium-high heat, sauté onions in 2 tablespoons oil until golden and caramelized. Add a drizzle of remaining oil to a separate skillet; cook a tortilla for 15 seconds on each side. Spoon onions, cheese and chicken onto half of tortilla; fold over and cook for about one minute, until light golden and crisp, or just until cheese melts for a soft quesadilla. Repeat with remaining ingredients. Makes 4 to 6 servings.

Whip up a zippy Tex-Mex side dish pronto! Prepare instant rice, using chicken broth instead of water. Stir in a generous dollop of spicy salsa, top with shredded cheese and cover until cheese melts.

Shrimp & Tomato Italiano

Rebecca Richardson
Boscawen, NH

Once when I was staying with my grandmother, we had a heavy snowstorm. I decided to make lunch with the ingredients we had on hand...this yummy dish was the result.

3 14-1/2 oz. cans diced
   tomatoes with Italian herbs
1 T. garlic, minced
1-1/4 lbs. cooked medium
   shrimp, tails removed

12-oz. pkg. refrigerated
   fettuccine pasta, uncooked
salt and pepper to taste

Combine tomatoes with juice and garlic in a deep skillet over medium heat. Add shrimp to skillet; bring to a boil. Add pasta, stirring to prevent sticking. (Do not cook pasta ahead of time, to avoid overcooking.) Boil pasta to desired doneness, 3 to 4 minutes. Remove from heat; toss to mix well. Add salt and pepper to taste. Makes 3 to 4 servings.

Thaw frozen shrimp quickly by placing the shrimp in a colander and running cold water over it...ready to cook!

Broccoli con Fettuccine

Jamie Plichta
North Huntingdon, PA

We enjoy this recipe as a meatless meal or a satisfying side dish.
Try it with fresh asparagus too.

2 T. oil
1/2 t. garlic salt
1/2 c. broccoli flowerets,
    chopped
2 T. butter

8-oz. pkg. fettuccine pasta,
    cooked
1/2 c. chicken broth
2 egg yolks, beaten

Heat oil with garlic salt in a skillet over medium-high heat. Add broccoli and stir-fry for several minutes. Add butter and cooked pasta; stir to coat pasta. Add broth and egg yolks. Cook and stir for an additional 2 minutes; serve. Makes 3 to 4 servings.

Pour vegetable oil into a plastic squeeze bottle. This makes it easy to drizzle oil just where it's needed, with no waste and no mess.

Lemony Skillet Chicken

Hope Davenport
Portland, TX

My husband doesn't usually care for anything with lemons,
but he loves this dish!

1 T. olive oil
2 T. butter, divided
4 boneless, skinless chicken
   breasts
2 T. all-purpose flour

2/3 c. chicken broth
3 T. lemon juice
1/2 t. salt
1 t. dried chives

Heat oil and one tablespoon butter in a skillet over medium heat. Coat chicken in flour and add to skillet. Sauté for about 6 minutes on each side, turning once, until chicken juices run clear. Remove chicken from skillet; keep warm. Add broth, lemon juice, salt and chives to skillet and bring to a boil. Remove from heat; stir in remaining butter. Return chicken to skillet and spoon sauce over chicken, turning to coat. Serves 4.

Don't toss that lemon half after it's been juiced! Wrap it and store in the freezer, ready to grate whenever a recipe calls for fresh lemon zest.

Cheesy Chicken-Tomato Pasta

Tonya Lewis
Crothersville, IN

*Scrumptious and so easy to fix, this skillet meal is quicker
than a boxed dinner helper!*

8-oz. pkg. radiatore or rotini
   pasta, uncooked and divided
3/4 lb. boneless chicken breast
   stir-fry strips
10-3/4 oz. can cream of
   chicken soup

1/2 c. milk
1-1/2 c. roma tomatoes,
   chopped
2 T. fresh basil, chopped
1 c. shredded mozzarella cheese

Measure 2 cups uncooked pasta and cook according to package
directions; drain. Reserve remaining pasta for another recipe.
Meanwhile, heat a non-stick skillet over medium-high heat. Add
chicken; cook for 4 to 6 minutes, stirring frequently, until no longer
pink in the center. Reduce heat to medium; stir in soup, milk,
tomatoes, basil and cooked pasta. Cook for about 8 minutes, stirring
occasionally, until bubbly and heated through. Sprinkle with cheese.
Remove from heat; cover and let stand until cheese is melted,
2 to 3 minutes. Serves 4.

When browning meat, don't overcrowd the skillet. Add meat
cubes or strips in batches, not all at once.

Easy Pork Chops & Rice

Pam Tallant
Lakewood, OH

For a complete meal, top with broccoli flowerets before covering the skillet. They'll be perfectly steamed when the pork chops are done.

4 pork chops
1 T. oil
salt and pepper to taste
10-3/4 oz. can French onion
   soup

1-1/4 c. water
1/2 c. celery, chopped
1/4 t. dried thyme
1/2 c. long-cooking rice,
   uncooked

In a skillet over medium heat, brown pork chops in oil. Drain; sprinkle to taste with salt and pepper. Add remaining ingredients; cover. Cook for 20 minutes longer, or until pork chops and rice are tender. Makes 4 servings.

Boneless chicken breasts and pork cutlets cook up faster if pounded thin with a meat mallet or even a small heavy skillet. Place meat in a large plastic zipping bag first for no-mess convenience.

SIZZLING *Skillets*

Skillet Surprise

*Linda Davidson
Lexington, KY*

*A speedy, budget-friendly dinner...canned corned beef, browned
and drained ground beef or sausage are all tasty. Sometimes
I'll even fix this using 8 scrambled eggs instead of the meat.*

1 to 2 T. olive oil
30-oz. pkg. frozen diced
   potatoes
1/2 onion, chopped
Optional: 1/2 green pepper,
   chopped

1 lb. cooked meat, chopped
8-oz. pkg. shredded Cheddar
   cheese

Heat oil in a large skillet over medium heat. Add potatoes, onion and
pepper, if using; cook according to package directions. When potatoes
are golden, add cooked meat; stir very well. Cover skillet; cook over
low heat until heated through. Sprinkle with cheese; cover and let
cheese melt. Serves 4 to 6.

Get out Grandma's cast-iron skillet for the tastiest stovetop
meals. Cast iron provides even heat distribution for speedy
cooking and crisp golden crusts. It can even be popped directly
into the oven or under a broiler to finish cooking.

Lomo Saltado

Patti Chandler
Dacula, GA

My sister-in-law married a Peruvian man and he loved this recipe.
It's hard to believe that it has been 40 years since
she first shared it with me!

3 to 4 T. oil, divided
4 to 5 potatoes, peeled and
   thinly sliced
2 lbs. beef flank steak, thinly
   sliced

salt and pepper to taste
2 tomatoes, diced
1 green pepper, sliced
1 onion, sliced
cooked rice

Heat 3 tablespoons oil in a large skillet over medium-high heat.
Cook potatoes until golden; drain and set aside. Add beef and more
oil, if necessary. Stir-fry until browned. Drain and remove from
skillet; sprinkle with salt and pepper and set aside. Add tomatoes,
green pepper and onion to skillet; stir-fry until crisp-tender. Return
meat mixture and potatoes to skillet; stir until well blended. Serve
with rice. Makes 4 servings.

Successful stir-frying depends on quick cooking at a high
temperature...be sure to have all your ingredients chopped
and sauces mixed up before you start!

Apricot-Glazed Pork Chops

Cindy Snavely
Gooseberry Patch

My neighbor, Betty, shared this recipe for tangy pork chops with me.
I like to serve them with rice pilaf and buttered baby carrots.

1/3 c. apricot preserves
1/3 c. white wine or apple juice
1/2 t. ground ginger

2 T. oil
4 pork chops
salt and pepper to taste

Mix preserves, wine or juice and ginger in a small bowl; set aside.
Heat oil in a large skillet over medium-high heat. Add pork chops;
sprinkle with salt and pepper. Cook until golden, about 4 minutes on
each side. Remove pork chops from skillet; keep warm. Turn down
heat to medium-low. Add preserves mixture to skillet and simmer
until thickened, about 4 minutes. Return pork chops to skillet. Cook
for about one minute on each side, until well coated with sauce.
Makes 4 servings.

Freeze uncooked chicken, beef
or pork cutlets with marinade
in freezer bags. After thawing
overnight in the fridge, meat
can go right into the skillet or
onto the grill for a savory meal.

Sweet-and-Sour Popcorn Chicken
Patricia Wissler
Harrisburg, PA

My grandsons love this meal! I always keep the ingredients on hand because I know they'll ask for it when they come to visit. Sometimes I also add a cup of sliced frozen carrots, thawed, to the skillet along with the pineapple.

20-oz. can pineapple tidbits,
   drained and juice reserved
3 T. white vinegar
2 T. soy sauce
2 T. catsup
1/3 to 1/2 c. brown sugar,
   packed
2 T. cornstarch

1 green pepper, sliced into
   1-inch pieces
1 onion, thinly sliced
1 T. oil
12-oz. pkg. frozen popcorn
   chicken
cooked rice

Combine reserved juice with enough water to measure 1-1/3 cups; add vinegar, soy sauce and catsup. In a separate bowl, combine brown sugar and cornstarch. Stir in juice mixture until smooth; set aside. In a large skillet over medium-high heat, stir-fry pepper and onion in oil for 3 to 4 minutes, or until crisp-tender. Gradually add juice mixture to skillet; bring to a boil. Cook and stir for 2 minutes, or until thickened. Add pineapple tidbits; reduce heat and simmer, uncovered, for 4 to 5 minutes, until heated through. Microwave chicken according to package directions. When hot, stir into pineapple mixture. Serve over cooked rice. Serves 4.

Unless a recipe specifies otherwise, canola oil is a good choice for stir-fries. It can stand up to high heat without smoking or burning.

SIZZLING *Skillets*

Spicy Pork Noodle Bowls

Brenda Smith
Gooseberry Patch

While on vacation, my teenage daughter loved this dish at an Oriental restaurant, so I just had to try and recreate it for her at home. She agrees I've succeeded!

8-oz. pkg. linguine pasta,
   uncooked
2 T. oil, divided
1 lb. boneless pork shoulder,
   sliced into strips
1 onion, thinly sliced
1/2 lb. broccoli, cut into
   bite-size flowerets

2 T. Worcestershire sauce
1 T. soy sauce
2 t. cornstarch
1/2 t. curry powder
1 tomato, chopped

Cook half of pasta according to package directions; set aside. Reserve remaining pasta for another recipe. Heat one tablespoon oil in a large skillet over high heat. Add pork; cook and stir until golden, about 7 minutes. Remove pork; set aside. Heat remaining oil in skillet; add onion and broccoli. Cook and stir until tender, about 5 minutes. Mix together sauces, cornstarch and curry powder in a cup; stir into skillet. Cook and stir until slightly thickened. Return pork to pan; heat through. Divide cooked pasta into 4 shallow bowls. Top with pork mixture and tomato; toss to coat pasta. Serves 4.

It's a snap to slice uncooked meat that has been slightly frozen...pop it in the freezer for 10 to 15 minutes first.

Creamy Shrimp Stir-Fry

Sasha Kelton
Henrietta, TX

A real time-saver for busy nights! Just remember to place the frozen shrimp and vegetables in the fridge to thaw the night before.

1 yellow onion, chopped
3 T. butter, divided
2 c. frozen stir-fry vegetables, thawed
garlic salt, seasoning salt and pepper to taste
1 lb. frozen cooked large shrimp, thawed and tails removed
3 T. milk
1/2 c. sour cream
cooked rice

In a large skillet over medium heat, sauté onion in one tablespoon butter until soft. Add vegetables and sprinkle to taste with seasonings. Add shrimp; cook until heated through. Remove shrimp mixture to a large bowl; set aside. Melt remaining butter in same skillet over low heat. Add milk and sour cream; mix well. Sprinkle lightly with garlic salt, seasoning salt and pepper. Return shrimp mixture to skillet; stir to coat with sauce. Serve over cooked rice. Makes 4 servings.

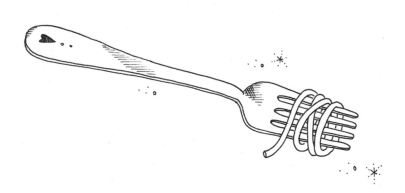

For a whole new taste that's thrifty too, add leftover spaghetti to any stir-fry supper. Cook and stir cold spaghetti in a little oil until heated through. Serve your stir-fry entree spooned over the warm spaghetti...yummy!

Stovetop Tuna Casserole

Tiffany Shaw
Clinton, WI

My Grandma Shaw passed this recipe on to my dad...it was the first meal he learned to make. When I was 9 years old, Dad taught me how to make it and it was the first meal that I had ever made, too. It's still my favorite comfort food.

1 onion, chopped
1/4 c. butter
6-oz. can tuna, drained
26-oz. can cream of
    mushroom soup
1-2/3 c. milk

1 c. frozen green peas
3 slices American cheese,
    chopped
salt and pepper
16-oz. pkg. small shell pasta,
    cooked

In a large skillet, sauté onion in butter until transparent but not browned. Add tuna, soup and milk; cook and stir until smooth. Add peas and cheese; stir frequently until hot and bubbly. Simmer for about 2 to 5 minutes, until peas are thawed; add salt and pepper to taste. Pour over cooked shells; mix well and serve. Makes 4 to 6 servings.

Post a notepad on the fridge to make a note whenever a pantry staple is used up...you'll never run out of that one item you need.

Potato & Ham Frittata

Eve Welch
Accokeek, MD

We love this quick & easy recipe for breakfast, lunch or dinner.

2 c. frozen hashbrowns with
   onions and peppers
3 T. butter
6 eggs

2 T. water
pepper to taste
1 c. cooked ham, diced

In a skillet over medium heat, cook hashbrowns in butter until golden, stirring occasionally. Whisk together eggs, water and pepper; stir in ham. Pour over hashbrowns in skillet. Cook over low heat for 9 to 10 minutes. As eggs set, run a spatula around edge of skillet, lifting edges to allow uncooked portion to flow underneath. Continue cooking and lifting edges until eggs are almost set. Remove from heat. Cover; let stand for 3 to 4 minutes before cutting into wedges. Serves 4.

Ham is so versatile for whipping up scrumptious quick meals! It's budget-friendly on supermarket holiday specials too. Why not pick up an extra to cut into cubes or slices and freeze in recipe-size portions. It'll be ready to add to casseroles and egg dishes at a moment's notice.

SIZZLING *Skillets*

Scrambled Mac & Cheese

Cheryl Barkalow
Germantown, OH

If you have leftover cooked macaroni on hand, just measure out 3 cups for this recipe.

8-oz. pkg. elbow macaroni, uncooked
1/2 lb. bacon

5 eggs, beaten
8 to 10 slices American cheese

Measure out 1-1/2 cups macaroni and cook according to package directions; set aside. Reserve remaining uncooked macaroni for another recipe. Fry bacon in a large skillet over medium heat until crisp. Drain; crumble bacon and return to skillet. Lower heat; add eggs, stirring to scramble. Add cooked macaroni, stirring well. Arrange cheese slices evenly over top of skillet mixture. Remove from heat; cover and let stand until cheese is melted. Serves 6.

It's a lovely thing...everyone sitting down together, sharing food.
-Alice May Brock

Creamed Chicken on Toast

Lynn Hedger
South Hutchinson, KS

This recipe is so simple, yet so good. My mom used to fix this at least once a week as it is easy and inexpensive...we always gobbled it up! It's simple to double or triple the recipe as needed.

1/4 c. butter
1/4 c. all-purpose flour
2 c. milk
2 4-1/2 oz. cans chicken,
   drained and flaked

1/2 t. salt
4 slices bread, toasted

Melt butter in a medium saucepan over medium-low heat; stir in flour. Add milk gradually, stirring vigorously. Bring to a boil; reduce heat. Add chicken and salt. Cook until heated through, stirring constantly; continue cooking and stirring for one minute longer. Serve over toast. Serves 2.

For a tasty change from toast and biscuits, whip up some crisp golden waffles to top with creamed tuna or chicken...yum!

Nutty Rice & Spinach Toss

*Lane McLoud
Siloam Springs, AR*

*I created this recipe for a rice contest and was one of five national
finalists. It can be enjoyed as either a meatless main or
a side dish that's delightfully different.*

1/3 c. butter
2 c. sliced mushrooms
3-oz. pkg. cream cheese,
   softened and cubed
3 c. cooked rice

2 c. spinach, torn
1/2 c. grated Parmesan cheese
1/2 c. chopped walnuts
1/4 t. salt
1/4 t. pepper

Melt butter in a large skillet over medium heat. Add mushrooms
and cook until soft, 2 to 4 minutes. Add cream cheese and stir until
melted. Reduce heat to medium-low; add cooked rice. Stir until
blended and heated through, 3 to 4 minutes. Remove from heat;
transfer mushroom mixture to a serving bowl. Add remaining
ingredients and toss well. Makes 4 to 6 servings.

Freeze leftover cooked rice for quick-fix meals later...just freeze
portions flat in plastic zipping bags. Use for stir-fry dishes,
to make soups thick & hearty or mix in fresh vegetables
for an easy side dish.

Ground Beef & Noodles

Billie Jean Elliott
Woodsfield, OH

Since I am a cookbook collector, everyone knows I love to try different recipes. This recipe was shared with me by a dear friend...
I hope you'll like it as much as I do!

1 lb. ground beef round
2 onions, diced
1 green pepper, diced
3/4 t. salt
3/4 t. pepper
3 c. cooked egg noodles

1-1/2 c. tomato juice
2 c. diced or stewed tomatoes
1-1/2 T. sugar
Optional: grated Parmesan
   cheese

Combine ground beef, onions, green pepper, salt and pepper in a skillet. Cook over medium heat until beef is browned; drain and set aside. Add cooked noodles, juice, tomatoes and sugar to beef mixture. Mix well and heat through; top with Parmesan cheese, if desired. Serves 6 to 8.

Keep ready-to-eat veggies like celery stalks, baby carrots and cherry tomatoes in the fridge for healthy snacking anytime.

Grandma Goldie's Sketti

Tamara Gallo
Bridgman, MI

This dish was a staple with all special meals at my Great-Grandma Goldie's house. The recipe has been passed down now to her great-great-grandchildren. It is very different and really good! Of course Goldie always had freshly brewed sun tea, so I recommend enjoying a tall glass along with your "sketti."

8-oz. pkg. pasteurized process
    cheese spread, cubed
2 c. stewed tomatoes in juice
1 to 2 T. sugar

1/4 t. celery seed
salt and pepper to taste
8-oz. pkg. spaghetti, cooked

Combine all ingredients except spaghetti in a medium saucepan. Cook over medium heat until cheese is almost melted, stirring constantly to prevent scorching. Use a wooden spoon to mash up tomatoes well. Remove from heat; toss in spaghetti and stir to coat well. Transfer to a serving platter. Serves 4.

Weekly theme nights make meal planning simple...have family members choose their favorites! They'll look forward to Spaghetti Monday and Tex-Mex Tuesday...you'll always know the answer to "What's for dinner?"

Husband-Pleasin' Dirty Rice

Cindy McKinnon
El Dorado, AR

This is my husband's favorite dish...mine too, because it's so easy!

1 lb. ground beef
1 lb. sage-flavored ground pork
   sausage
1/2 c. onion, chopped
1/2 c. celery, chopped
3 c. water
3 c. instant rice, uncooked

Brown beef, sausage, onion and celery in a skillet over medium heat. Drain; add water and bring to a boil. Add rice and stir very well. Remove from heat; cover and let stand for 5 minutes. Stir again and serve. Serves 6 to 8.

Cook rice in chicken or beef broth instead of plain water... an oh-so-easy way to add flavor.

SIZZLING *Skillets*

Grandma's Hot Dog Skillet Meal

Jeannie Beck
Hillsborough, NC

My mother-in-law gave me this recipe...my husband had always loved it as a kid and he still does. It's a different way to serve hot dogs. Our daughter enjoyed it while growing up and now she and her family are enjoying it together too.

8-oz. pkg. medium egg noodles,
   uncooked
6 hot dogs, sliced into 1/2-inch
   pieces
2 T. margarine
4 c. diced tomatoes

1 T. dried, minced onion
1/2 T. sugar
1/2 t. garlic powder
1/2 t. salt
Optional: grated Parmesan
   cheese

Cook half the noodles according to package directions; drain. Reserve remaining noodles for another recipe. In a large skillet over medium heat, brown hot dogs in margarine. Stir in cooked noodles and remaining ingredients except Parmesan cheese; bring to a boil. Reduce heat and simmer for 20 minutes, stirring occasionally. Sprinkle with Parmesan cheese, if desired. Serves 6.

Make up some handy file cards listing the ingredients needed for your most-used dinner recipes..shopping will be a breeze!

Chicken-Broccoli Stir-Fry

Tobi Taiwo
Ontario, Canada

My aunt made this for me once and it tasted so good! Ever since then,
I've tried making it her way...I think I finally have it right.

2 to 3 T. oil
2 cloves garlic, finely chopped
1/2 bunch broccoli, cut into
   bite-size pieces
1 carrot, peeled and cut into
   bite-size pieces
1 red pepper, cut into bite-size
   pieces
1 green pepper, cut into
   bite-size pieces

1 onion, cut into bite-size pieces
3 boneless, skinless chicken
   breasts, sliced into bite-size
   pieces
2 to 4 t. chicken broth or water,
   divided
1 t. curry powder
1/2 t. salt
cooked rice

Place oil and garlic in a large skillet over medium heat; cook until garlic is tender. Add vegetables and chicken; sprinkle with 2 teaspoons broth or water, curry powder and salt. Cook and stir for 10 minutes, adding remaining broth or water if needed. Serve over cooked rice. Makes 5 to 6 servings.

Slice stir-fry meat and veggies into equal-size pieces...
they'll all be cooked to perfection at the same time.

TOSS-TOGETHER Suppers

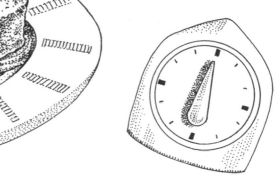

Stuffed Chicken Breasts

Ursala Armstrong
Odenville, AL

*Simple yet elegant...good enough for drop-in guests! Grill some
asparagus spears along with the chicken for a simple side.*

4 boneless, skinless chicken
   breasts
8-oz. container garlic & herb
  cream cheese spread

8 slices bacon

Flatten chicken breasts between wax paper. Spread each chicken
breast with cream cheese and roll up. Wrap 2 slices bacon around
each roll; secure with toothpicks. Place on a grill or in a grill pan over
medium heat. Cook, turning occasionally, until golden and chicken
juices run clear, about 20 to 25 minutes. Serves 4.

When chopping onions or celery, it only takes a moment
to chop a little extra. Tuck them away in the freezer
for a quick start to dinner another day.

Golden Breaded Pork Chops

Elizabeth Mullett
Wilmington, MA

*A quick-cooking two-in-one recipe that I created one day when
I bought a pork roast on sale. The second night, you just need to
reheat the pork chops and sauce while the pasta is cooking!*

1/2 c. dry bread crumbs
1/4 c. grated Parmesan cheese
1 T. dried oregano
1 t. dried marjoram
2 eggs, beaten

3-1/2 lb. boneless center-cut
  pork roast, sliced into
  1-1/2 inch chops
1/2 c. olive oil
salt and pepper to taste

Mix bread crumbs, Parmesan cheese and herbs in a shallow bowl; set
aside. Beat eggs in a separate bowl. Dip pork chops into egg, then into
crumb mixture, reserving any remaining crumb mixture. Heat oil in
a deep skillet over medium-low heat. Cook chops for 5 to 7 minutes
on each side until golden, adding salt and pepper to taste. If desired,
follow directions below to prepare a second meal. Makes two meals,
5 servings each.

Pork Chops & Tomatoes:

The first night, serve 5 pork chops, one per person. To pork chops
remaining in skillet, add remaining crumb mixture, one 28-ounce can
diced tomatoes and two, 14-1/2 ounce cans diced tomatoes with basil,
garlic and oregano. Reduce heat to low and simmer while the family
is eating dinner. Refrigerate chops and sauce. The second night, cut
chops into cubes; stir back into sauce and heat through. Serve over
cooked pasta of your choice.

A quick & easy seasoning mix is
six parts salt to one part pepper. Keep
it close to the stove in a large shaker...
so handy when pan-frying pork chops
or chicken.

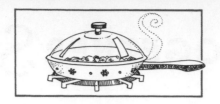

Speedy Skillet Lasagna

Tami Bowman
Gooseberry Patch

My family agrees that this is yummy! It's really fast to fix too...
you don't even need to precook the pasta.

1 lb. ground turkey
1/4 t. garlic powder
1/4 t. Italian seasoning
2 14-oz. cans beef broth
   with onion
14-1/2 oz. can diced tomatoes

8-oz. pkg. rotini pasta,
   uncooked and divided
1/2 c. shredded mozzarella
   cheese
Garnish: 1/4 c. grated Parmesan
   cheese

In a skillet over medium heat, brown ground turkey; drain and add seasonings. Stir in broth and tomatoes with juice; heat to boiling. Add 2 cups uncooked rotini; reserve remaining rotini for another recipe. Cover skillet; cook over medium heat for 12 to 14 minutes, until rotini is tender. Stir in mozzarella cheese; top each serving with Parmesan cheese. Serves 4 to 5.

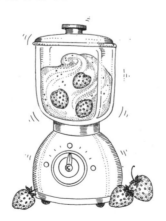

Whip up some fruit smoothies for a healthy before-dinner snack. Fill a blender with your favorite fresh or frozen fruit... strawberries and bananas are especially luscious! Add fruit juice or yogurt to taste. Process until smooth and garnish with a sprig of fresh mint.

Favorite Hamburger Goulash

Patty Trantham
Linwood, NC

When I was first married, this was a favorite for my husband and me. It is very inexpensive and makes enough to enjoy leftovers a second night. Topped with cheeses and baked, it tastes like a different dish altogether! Now, as we are older, these are still two of our favorite meals.

1 to 1-1/2 lbs. lean ground beef
1 onion, chopped
8-oz. pkg. elbow macaroni,
   cooked

32-oz. can diced tomatoes
10-3/4 oz. can tomato soup
6-oz. can tomato paste
2 c. water

Place ground beef and onion in a large frying pan. Brown over medium heat; drain. Stir in remaining ingredients. Bring to a boil, stirring occasionally to prevent sticking, until hot. Serve immediately, reserving half for a second meal; cover and refrigerate. Makes 2 meals of 2 to 3 servings each.

Cheesy Goulash Bake:

To give remaining goulash a little twist, spoon into lightly greased individual casserole dishes. Sprinkle with garlic salt to taste; bake, uncovered, at 325 degrees for 10 minutes. Top with shredded Cheddar and mozzarella cheese as desired. Bake for an additional 5 minutes, until heated through and cheese is bubbly.

Oops! If a simmering pot starts to burn on the bottom,
don't worry. Spoon the unburnt portion into another pan, being
careful not to scrape up the scorched part on the bottom.
The burnt taste usually won't linger.

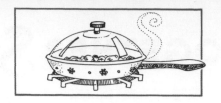

Balsamic Chicken & Rice

Dana Toy
Kittanning, PA

*This recipe is something I made up one day when I was in a hurry
to cook dinner. I used ingredients I had on hand and presto,
a family favorite was born!*

1 onion, sliced
2 T. olive oil
4 boneless, skinless chicken
  breasts

1 c. balsamic & basil vinaigrette
  salad dressing
14-1/2 oz. can diced tomatoes
2 c. cooked rice

Sauté onion with oil in a skillet over medium heat. Add chicken;
cook until golden on both sides. Top chicken with salad dressing and
tomatoes in juice. Reduce heat; cover and simmer for 20 minutes,
until chicken juices run clear. Serve chicken and sauce over cooked
rice. Serves 4.

Chicken thighs are extra flavorful and easy on the budget, but
are usually sold with the bone in. To speed up cooking time,
use a sharp knife to make a deep cut on each side of the bone.

TOSS-TOGETHER Suppers

Savory Chicken Stew

Vickie

*I love to serve this scrumptious stew with crusty bread
to soak up all the flavorful juices.*

1 onion, chopped
1 green pepper, chopped
1 T. oil
1/2 c. all-purpose flour
1/4 t. onion powder
1/4 t. paprika

1/4 t. salt
1/4 t. pepper
2 lbs. boneless, skinless
   chicken, cubed
8-oz. can tomato sauce
1/2 c. chicken broth

In a large skillet over medium heat, sauté onion and green pepper in
oil until soft, about 5 minutes. Remove onion and pepper from skillet;
set aside. Mix flour and seasonings in a large plastic zipping bag.
Add chicken cubes; close bag and shake to coat chicken. Transfer
chicken to skillet; cook until golden on both sides. Return onion
and pepper to skillet; stir in sauce and broth. Cover and simmer for
10 to 15 minutes, until chicken is done. Makes 4 to 6 servings.

Cutting down on fat? Spray your skillet with non-stick
vegetable spray before sautéing chopped onions,
celery and other vegetables.

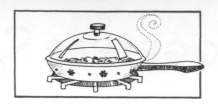

Hodge Podge

Sabrina Lawrence
Manor, TX

My college roommate's mom served this one weekend when we went home for a visit. I have made it ever since for my family and they love it too. It's a great change from chili for chilly-weather days...oh-so easy and yummy!

1 lb. ground beef or turkey
14-1/2 oz. can diced tomatoes
   with chiles

15-oz. can ranch-style beans
19-oz. can minestrone soup
cooked rice

Brown meat in a skillet over medium heat; drain. Add tomatoes with chiles, beans and soup; simmer for 20 minutes. Serve over cooked rice. Serves 6.

Place browned ground beef in a colander and run hot water over it. Excess fat will rinse right off, with no loss in flavor.

TOSS-TOGETHER Suppers

Stacey's Not Soup

Renee Angil
Dayton, OH

When my husband and I were stationed in Japan, we had our first son. Unfortunately he was born very ill, and he spent a month getting better in a Japanese hospital. Some of our dear friends got together and brought us meals each night. One of my favorites was this recipe. When I called my friend Stacey to thank her for her "soup," she laughed and said it wasn't supposed to be "soup"...ever since then, I just refer to it as Stacey's Not Soup!

1 lb. Kielbasa, sliced
14-1/2 oz. can beef broth
2 zucchini, sliced
2 yellow squash, sliced
1 pt. grape tomatoes

3 green onions, sliced
2 t. dried basil
16-oz. pkg. penne pasta, cooked
1 T. olive oil

Combine Kielbasa and broth in a large skillet. Bring to a boil over medium heat; turn down heat and simmer for about 5 minutes. Add vegetables; cook until tender. Stir in basil. Toss cooked pasta with oil; serve sauce over pasta. Serves 4 to 6.

A flexible plastic cutting mat makes speedy work
of slicing & dicing. Keep two mats on hand
for chopping meat and veggies separately.

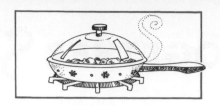

Roma Burgers on Spaghetti

Marlene Burns
Swisher, IA

Even kids can get tired of hamburgers! This recipe makes a tasty change from burgers served on buns.

6 T. dry bread crumbs
1/3 c. onion, chopped
1/3 c. green pepper, chopped
1 clove garlic, minced
salt and pepper to taste
6 T. grated Parmesan cheese,
  divided

1 lb. ground beef
16-oz. can tomato sauce
3/4 t. Italian seasoning
8-oz. pkg. spaghetti, cooked

Combine bread crumbs, onion, green pepper, garlic, salt, pepper and 3 tablespoons Parmesan cheese. Add ground beef; mix well and form into 6 burgers. Brown in a large skillet over medium-high heat for 2 minutes on each side. Combine sauce and seasoning; pour over burgers. Reduce heat; cover and simmer for 10 minutes. Serve burgers and sauce over cooked spaghetti, sprinkled with remaining cheese. Serves 6.

A big chalkboard in the kitchen is a handy spot
for a running grocery list.

TOSS-TOGETHER *Suppers*

Italian Sausage Salad

Rosemary Paul
Roxbury, CT

My 93-year-old mother-in-law always used to make this hearty salad for us in the summertime. Now that she is living in a nursing home, I am so glad that she shared the recipe with me many years ago, so I can continue to make it for my family.

1 lb. hot or sweet Italian pork
    sausage links
16-oz. pkg. cheese tortellini,
    cooked
2 green peppers, or 1 red pepper
    and 1 green pepper, chopped

2 onions, chopped
1 zucchini, sliced and cut into
    2-inch sticks
3.8-oz. can sliced black olives,
    drained
3 T. fresh parsley, chopped

Remove sausage casings and chop sausage. Brown in a skillet; drain. Combine sausage with remaining ingredients in a large serving bowl. Pour dressing over top; toss to mix and serve at room temperature. Makes 6 to 8 servings.

Dressing:

2/3 c. olive oil
3 T. wine vinegar
1 clove garlic, chopped

1/2 T. dried oregano
1/4 t. salt
1/4 t. pepper

Whisk all ingredients together.

When whipping up a speedy supper, use a kitchen timer...
let it watch the clock so you don't have to.

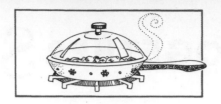

Sausage & Pepper Bake

Sherri White
Jacksonville, FL

My mom has been fixing this for many years...it tastes like stuffed peppers, but easier. My husband and I both enjoy it.

1-lb. pkg. ground pork sausage	1/4 c. dried, minced onion
14-oz. can tomato sauce	1-1/3 c. water
14-1/2 oz. can diced tomatoes	salt and pepper to taste
1/2 c. green pepper, chopped	1 c. instant rice, uncooked
1/2 c. red pepper, chopped	

Brown sausage in a skillet over medium heat; drain. Add remaining ingredients except rice. Simmer for about 15 minutes. When mixture boils, stir in rice. Remove from heat; cover and let stand for about 10 minutes. Stir before serving. Serves 6.

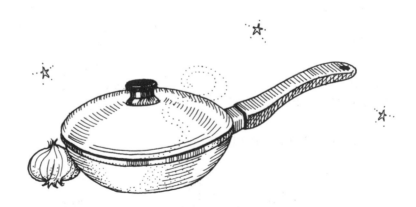

If your favorite non-stick skillet is sticky, fill it with one cup water, 1/2 cup vinegar and 2 tablespoons baking soda. Bring to a boil for a few minutes. Rinse well with hot water and wipe clean...no more stickiness!

One-Pot Sausage Etouffee

Laura Witham
Anchorage, AK

*I am from Wichita, Kansas and currently living in Anchorage, Alaska.
My passion is Cajun food and my favorite dish is etouffee. After several
tries, I have perfected a version of my own. When I ran a small food
ministry in Wichita, this was my most-requested recipe. I hope you love
it just as much!*

1/4 c. olive oil
1/4 c. all-purpose flour
1-lb. pkg. Kielbasa or smoked
   sausage ring, cut into
   bite-size pieces
1 onion, chopped
1 green pepper, chopped
4 cloves garlic, minced

1 T. Italian seasoning
salt and pepper to taste
2 14-1/2 oz. cans diced
   tomatoes
4 cubes beef bouillon
4 c. water
2 c. long-cooking rice, uncooked

Pour oil and flour into a stockpot over medium-low heat. Cook and
stir constantly until mixture is deep brown. Add Kielbasa or sausage,
onion, green pepper, garlic and seasonings to stockpot. Simmer,
stirring occasionally, for 5 minutes. Add tomatoes with juice, bouillon,
water and uncooked rice; bring to a boil. Turn heat to low; cover and
simmer until rice has absorbed all the liquid. Taste before serving; add
more salt and pepper, if desired. Makes 4 to 5 servings.

No fresh garlic in the pantry? Substitute 1/8 teaspoon garlic
powder for each clove of garlic needed...moisten it with
a little water first to brighten its flavor.

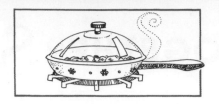

Jill's Spicy Tomato Pasta

Heather Porter
Villa Park, IL

My 12-year-old daughter, Jill, has been watching lots of cooking shows on TV and she wanted to develop her own special pasta sauce recipe. After a visit to the grocery store, she came up with this easy, very delicious recipe all on her own!

26-oz. jar tomato & spicy red pepper pasta sauce
1/4 c. water
6-oz. can tomato paste
14-1/2 oz. can chicken broth
8-oz. container whipping cream
6 leaves fresh basil, chopped
favorite pasta, cooked
Garnish: grated Parmesan cheese

Pour sauce into a large saucepan. Add water to jar and shake to get all of the sauce out; pour into saucepan. Stir in tomato paste and broth; simmer over medium-low heat for 15 minutes. Just before serving, stir in cream and basil; mix well. Serve over cooked pasta. Sprinkle with Parmesan cheese, as desired. Serves 4.

Cooking up an extra-quick spaghetti dinner? Choose angel hair pasta...it takes just three minutes to cook, once the water is boiling.

TOSS-TOGETHER Suppers

Italian Chicken Spaghetti

Lydia Edgy
Knoxville, TN

My best friend, Jenny, shared this with me. We no longer live close to one another, but every time I make this I think of her.

1 c. Italian-flavored dry bread
    crumbs
4 boneless, skinless chicken
    breasts, halved
2 t. olive oil

16-oz. pkg. spaghetti, uncooked
4 c. chicken broth
Garnish: grated Parmesan
    cheese

Place bread crumbs into a large plastic zipping bag. Moisten chicken with a little water and place into bag with crumbs; shake until chicken is coated. Heat oil in a large skillet over medium heat. Add chicken to skillet; cook until golden and juices run clear. While chicken is cooking, boil spaghetti in broth for 8 to 10 minutes, until tender; drain. Serve chicken over spaghetti, sprinkled with Parmesan cheese. Serves 4.

Wrap up leftover dinner rolls and freeze, then grate while still frozen to use in any recipe that calls for bread crumbs.

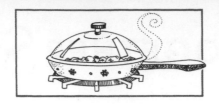

Country Pork Chop Dinner

*Crystal Young
Danville, KY*

*This hearty one-pot recipe is one of the first meals I prepared after
I got married...it's still one of our favorites.*

4 pork chops
1 onion, chopped
1 T. oil
4 redskin potatoes, cubed
1 c. carrots, peeled and sliced
4-1/2 oz. jar sliced mushrooms,
    drained

10-3/4 oz. can cream of celery
    soup
1/2 c. water
3/4 t. dried thyme
1 t. salt

In a large skillet over medium heat, brown pork chops and onion in
oil. Drain; add potatoes, carrots and mushrooms. Mix together soup,
water, thyme and salt; add to skillet. Bring all to a boil. Reduce heat;
cover and simmer for 30 minutes, until pork chops and vegetables are
tender. Serves 4.

A squeaky-clean stovetop...
no elbow grease required!
Cover baked-on food spots
with equal parts water and
baking soda and let the food
soak right off.

Beef & Rice Hot Pot

Susan Dickinson
Prentice, WI

I combined several quick-fix recipes to come up with this one.
Try it sometime with two cups of leftover cooked, chopped chicken
instead of the ground beef.

1 lb. ground beef
1 onion, chopped
2 stalks celery, chopped
salt and pepper to taste
1/2 c. long-cooking brown rice,
    uncooked
1/2 c. long-cooking white rice,
    uncooked

10-3/4 oz. can cream of chicken
    soup
6 T. soy sauce
2-1/2 c. water
Garnish: chow mein noodles

Brown ground beef, onion and celery in a large skillet over medium heat; drain. Add salt and pepper to taste. Stir in remaining ingredients except noodles; bring to a boil. Reduce heat; cover and simmer for 20 minutes, or until liquid is absorbed. Top servings with noodles. Serves 4 to 6.

Use a potato masher to break up ground beef quickly
and evenly as it browns.

Skillet Macaroni & Cheese

Michelle Taggart
Parker, CO

I first made this recipe back in high school. It's wonderful for summer days when you don't want to heat up the kitchen by turning on the oven.

1/2 c. butter
8-oz. pkg. elbow macaroni,
　uncooked and divided
1/2 c. onion, chopped
1/2 c. green pepper, chopped
1-1/4 t. salt
1/4 t. pepper

1/4 t. dry mustard
2 c. water
1 T. all-purpose flour
8-oz. pkg. shredded Cheddar
　cheese
12-oz. can evaporated milk

Melt butter in a skillet over low heat. Add 2 cups uncooked macaroni, onion, green pepper and seasonings; cook until onion is transparent. (Reserve remaining uncooked macaroni for another recipe.) Add water; stir and bring to a boil. Cover and simmer for 20 minutes, or until tender. Sprinkle flour over macaroni mixture and blend in; stir in cheese and evaporated milk. Continue to simmer for 5 minutes at low temperature, or until cheese melts. Makes 4 to 6 servings.

No matter what looms ahead, if you can eat today, enjoy today, mix good cheer with friends today, enjoy it and bless God for it.
-Henry Ward Beecher

Zesty Penne & Peppers

Lisa Bowers
Harmony, PA

If you like peppers, you'll love this dish!

1-lb. pkg. ground hot
  pork sausage
14-oz. jar banana pepper rings
7-oz. jar roasted red peppers,
  drained and diced

16-oz. pkg. penne pasta,
  uncooked
3-1/2 c. hot water
8-oz. container whipping cream
3/4 c. grated Parmesan cheese

In a large skillet over medium heat, cook sausage until browned;
drain. Chop up sausage as desired and return to skillet. Remove half
of banana peppers from jar; drain and dice, reserving remaining
banana peppers for another recipe. Add diced banana peppers,
roasted red peppers, uncooked pasta and hot water to skillet; stir.
Bring to a boil over medium-high heat. Cover and cook for about
12 to 15 minutes, or until pasta is tender and most of the water has
evaporated. Pour cream and cheese over pasta mixture. Mix until well
blended and serve. Makes 4 to 6 servings.

Add some fresh broccoli, asparagus or snow peas to a favorite
pasta recipe...simply drop chopped veggies into the pasta pot
about halfway through the cooking time. Pasta and veggies
will be tender at about the same time.

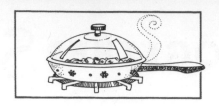

Chicken Alfredo Florentine

Lorrie Smith
Drummonds, TN

I enjoyed a dish similar to this at a restaurant and decided to see if I could duplicate it at home. This is what I came up with...I think it turned out pretty good!

8-oz. pkg. fettuccine pasta, uncooked
2 T. butter, sliced
17-oz. jar Alfredo pasta sauce
10-oz. pkg. frozen chopped spinach, thawed and drained

6-oz. pkg. grilled chicken strips
Garnish: grated Parmesan cheese

Cook pasta according to package directions; drain well and toss with butter. In a large saucepan, combine pasta, sauce, spinach and chicken. Simmer over low heat for about 15 minutes, until heated through. Sprinkle with Parmesan cheese and serve. Makes 4 servings.

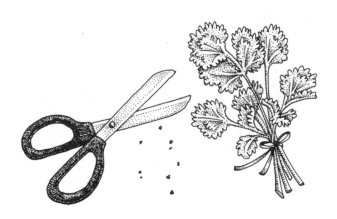

Keep a pair of kitchen scissors nearby for snipping fresh herbs and opening packages...you'll wonder what you ever did without them!

TOSS-TOGETHER *Suppers*

Cheddar Spaghetti

Amy Komara
Crystal River, FL

The kids and I concocted this one day when we didn't feel like running out to the grocery...it's definitely a fast, kid-friendly, comfort food! Those who can't eat tomatoes, or simply don't care for tomato-based spaghetti sauces, will find this to their liking too.

16-oz. pkg. spaghetti, uncooked
8-oz. pkg. shredded Cheddar
   cheese
2 T. butter

1/2 c. milk
1-lb. pkg. mild ground pork
   sausage, browned and
   drained

Coarsely break spaghetti, if desired. Cook spaghetti according to package directions; drain and return to pot. Add cheese and butter; stir until melted. Remove from heat. Add milk and sausage; stir until well blended. Serves 8.

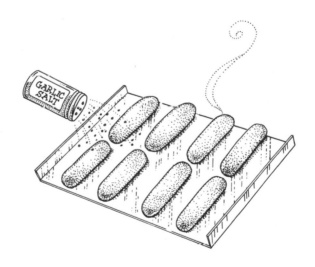

Turn hot dog buns into garlic bread sticks in a jiffy!
Spread with softened butter, sprinkle with garlic salt
and broil until toasty...yum!

Chicken Presto

Kathy Grashoff
Fort Wayne, IN

Why settle for take-out when you can serve up an Italian restaurant meal in less than 30 minutes?

2 T. oil
3 c. sliced mushrooms
1 onion, chopped
15-oz. can stewed tomatoes
1/4 c. Italian salad dressing
3 T. tomato paste

4 boneless, skinless chicken
  breasts
1 c. shredded mozzarella cheese
2 slices bacon, crisply cooked
  and crumbled

Heat oil in a large skillet over medium-high heat. Add mushrooms and onion; cook for 5 minutes, stirring occasionally. Stir in tomatoes with juice, salad dressing and tomato paste. Add chicken and cover; reduce heat to medium-low. Simmer for about 12 minutes, or until chicken is cooked through. Sprinkle with cheese and bacon; simmer, uncovered, for 5 minutes longer. Serves 4.

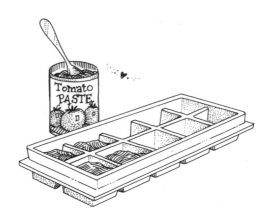

Don't let a drop of flavorful tomato paste go to waste!
If a recipe calls for just a partial can, spoon the rest
into ice cube trays and freeze for later use.

TOSS-TOGETHER *Suppers*

Mexican Chicken Olé

Vanessa McAlexander
Orlando, FL

My family loves this recipe and asks for me to fix it very often.
It's so easy that I'm happy to do so!

1 t. olive oil
4 boneless, skinless chicken
   breasts
salt and pepper to taste
15-1/4 oz. can corn, drained
15-oz. can black beans, drained
   and rinsed

14-1/2 oz. can diced tomatoes
   with chiles
1 c. shredded Cheddar cheese
Optional: cooked yellow rice

Heat oil in a frying pan over medium heat. Add chicken breasts;
sprinkle with salt and pepper to taste. Brown chicken for 3 to
4 minutes on each side. Top chicken with corn, black beans and
tomatoes with chiles; do not stir. Cover pan and cook over medium-
low heat for 15 to 20 minutes. Uncover; top with cheese. Turn heat
to low and cook for an additional 5 minutes, until cheese melts. Serve
with cooked rice, if desired. Serves 4.

Protect non-stick skillets from scratching when stacked in a
cupboard...slip a paper plate or coffee filter in between them.

Moira's Marinara Sauce

Alysson Marshall
Newark, NY

Wednesday night was always "pasta night" at our house when I was growing up. We had a large family so my mom made this quick & easy sauce with items she usually had on hand. I have carried on her tradition and now my family enjoys Wednesday pasta night too.

29-oz. can crushed tomatoes
6-oz. can tomato paste
1 T. dried basil

1 T. dried oregano
1 t. garlic powder

Mix all ingredients in a medium saucepan. Bring to a boil over medium heat. Reduce heat and simmer for about 30 minutes, stirring occasionally. Makes about 4 cups sauce.

Prevent messy pasta boil-overs! Rub a little vegetable oil over the top few inches inside the cooking pot.

TOSS-TOGETHER *Suppers*

Antipasto-Style Linguine

JoAnn

*A delicious combination of flavors and textures
that's quickly tossed together.*

12-oz. pkg. linguine pasta,
  uncooked
16-oz. jar antipasto salad
  with olives
3 T. olive oil
4 lg. portabella mushroom
  caps, sliced

6-oz. pkg. sliced deli salami,
  cut into thin strips
2 c. shredded Asiago cheese,
  divided
2 c. fresh basil, chopped
  and divided
pepper to taste

Cook pasta and drain, reserving 1/2 cup cooking water; set aside.
Measure one cup antipasto salad vegetables and 6 tablespoons
marinade from jar; reserve remainder for another recipe. Slice
vegetables and set aside. Heat oil in pasta pot over medium-high heat.
Sauté mushrooms until tender, about 6 minutes. Add salami; cook and
stir briefly. Add pasta, reserved cooking water, vegetables, reserved
marinade and 1-1/2 cups cheese; toss until liquid thickens and coats
pasta, about 3 minutes. Stir in 1-1/2 cups basil; add pepper to taste.
Garnish with remaining basil and cheese. Serves 4 to 6.

Did you know? For flavorful, fat-free sautés, you can substitute
broth for oil...just watch it carefully so food doesn't burn or stick.

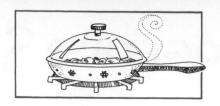

Connie's Skillet Meatloaf

Connie Wietjes
Gibbon, NE

This meatloaf is so simple and very good! Serve with hot buttered rolls and tangy coleslaw and you have a quick, hearty meal. I have been making this since I was in high school (that's been a few years now!) for my brothers and sisters and now for my own family.

2 lbs. lean ground beef
2 eggs, beaten
1 sleeve saltine crackers, crushed

1 potato, peeled and shredded
1 carrot, peeled and shredded
15-oz. can tomato sauce, divided

Mix all ingredients together, reserving half of tomato sauce. Pat into a lightly greased electric skillet. Pour reserved sauce over meatloaf. Cook, uncovered, for 10 minutes at 350 degrees; cover and simmer an additional 15 to 25 minutes. Or, simply pat into a greased skillet and cook on stovetop over medium heat, as directed. Serves 6.

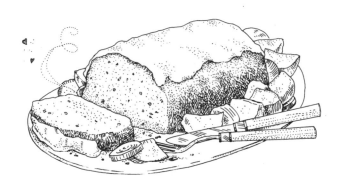

Stir cubes of leftover meatloaf into spaghetti sauce and serve over noodles...a tasty meal in minutes!

TOSS-TOGETHER Suppers

Ground Beef Stroganoff

Jennifer Crisp
Abingdon, IL

This recipe serves a family of 5 well, with no leftovers. My picky eaters never turn it down!

1 lb. ground beef
1/2 c. onion, sliced
1 T. garlic, chopped
1 t. paprika
1/2 c. beef broth
10-3/4 oz. can cream of
   mushroom soup

1-1/2 T. Worcestershire sauce
4-oz. can chopped mushrooms,
   drained
1/2 c. sour cream
1/3 c. milk
16-oz. pkg. egg noodles, cooked
   and buttered

Combine ground beef, onion, garlic and paprika in a skillet. Brown over medium heat; drain. Stir in broth, soup, sauce and mushrooms; simmer for one to 2 minutes. Add sour cream and milk; simmer for a few minutes, until hot. Serve over buttered egg noodles. Serves 5.

Take advantage of grocery specials on ground beef for easy, economical family meals! Crumble several pounds of beef onto a baking pan and bake at 350 degrees until browned through, stirring often. Drain well and pack recipe portions in freezer bags.

Zucchini & Beef in Wine Sauce

Beckie Butcher
Elgin, IL

*My own creation! It's very versatile...try it with chicken and
white wine or chicken broth.*

2 to 3 T. olive oil, divided
1 lb. stew beef, cubed
2 cloves garlic, minced
1 onion, sliced
1 zucchini, halved lengthwise
   and sliced into crescents

1/2 yellow pepper, chopped
1 red pepper, chopped
salt and pepper to taste
2-1/2 t. red wine or beef broth
Optional: grated Parmesan
   cheese

Heat 2 tablespoons oil in a frying pan over medium heat; brown meat.
Add garlic and sauté. Stir in onion, zucchini and peppers; mix well
and add salt and pepper to taste. Cook for about 15 to 20 minutes,
adding more oil as needed. Stir in wine or broth. If desired, sprinkle
with Parmesan cheese before serving. Serves 4.

Keep cutting boards smelling fresh by simply rubbing them
thoroughly with lemon wedges...it works for hands too!

Chicken in the Garden

*Summer Pieper
Kearney, MO*

*A fix & forget meal featuring pantry staples. Choose instant
brown rice to add whole-grain goodness, if you wish.*

4 boneless, skinless chicken
  breasts, sliced into strips
1 T. oil
14-1/2 oz. can French-cut green
  beans, drained
4-oz. can sliced mushrooms,
  drained

1 t. garlic salt
salt and pepper to taste
14-1/2 oz. can chicken broth
1 t. dried basil
1-1/2 c. instant rice, uncooked
Optional: soy sauce to taste

In a skillet over medium heat, brown chicken in oil. Stir in green
beans, mushrooms, garlic salt, salt and pepper. Add broth and basil;
bring to a boil. Stir in uncooked rice. Turn to low heat; cover and cook
for 15 minutes, or until broth is absorbed and rice is cooked. Sprinkle
with soy sauce, if desired. Serves 4 to 6.

Pick up a bottle of flavorful sesame oil for drizzling over
quick-cooked veggies, chicken and pork along
with soy sauce. Tasty!

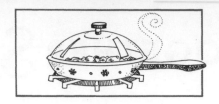

Basil Chicken Skillet

Emily Calhoun
Berne, IN

*I found this recipe in an old newspaper and added my own touches
to it. With a crisp tossed salad, it's a light and comforting meal
that's super-easy to make.*

2 boneless, skinless chicken
   breasts, diced
2 t. garlic, minced
1 onion, chopped
1 to 2 T. oil
14-oz. can diced tomatoes

2 c. chicken broth
1 t. dried basil, crushed
1/4 t. pepper
8-oz. pkg. spaghetti, uncooked
   and broken in half
1/4 c. grated Parmesan cheese

In a large skillet over medium heat, cook chicken, garlic and onion
in oil until chicken is golden and onion is tender. Add tomatoes
with juice, broth, basil and pepper to skillet. Bring to a boil. Stir in
spaghetti, making sure spaghetti is covered by liquid. Reduce heat;
cover and simmer for 15 to 20 minutes, until spaghetti is tender and
chicken is no longer pink. Sprinkle with Parmesan cheese and serve.
Serves 4.

Stock up on favorite canned vegetables when they're on sale...
they're oh-so handy when whipping up fast-fix meals.
Jot the purchase date on cans with a permanent marker
to keep pantry supplies rotated.

JUST Pop IN THE Oven

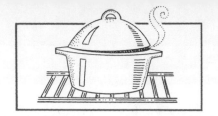

Hearty Shepherd's Pie

Cathy Armstrong
Limestone, TN

*This recipe takes just a short time to prepare. My family loves
the cheesy mashed potato topping.*

2 lbs. lean ground beef
1 sweet onion, chopped
1 green pepper, chopped
11-oz. can corn, plain or with
  diced peppers, drained

8 servings instant potato flakes,
  prepared
16-oz. pkg. shredded Cheddar
  cheese

In a large skillet over medium heat, brown meat with onion, pepper
and corn; drain. Spread over bottom of a lightly greased 13"x9" baking
pan. Spread prepared potatoes evenly over meat mixture; sprinkle
cheese over top. Bake, uncovered, at 350 degrees for 15 minutes,
or until cheese melts. Let stand for a few minutes; cut into squares
and serve. Serves 8.

When baking a casserole in a clear glass baking pan,
reduce your oven temperature by 25 degrees...
food cooks faster in glass pans than in metal.

Cowpoke Casserole

Debbie Hutchinson
Spring, TX

A cast-iron skillet is perfect...it can go right into the oven to bake.
Otherwise, transfer ground beef mixture to a casserole dish
before adding the cornbread batter.

1 lb. ground beef	8-oz. can tomato sauce
1/2 onion, chopped	1/2 c. water
salt and pepper to taste	8-1/2 oz. pkg. cornbread mix
1 t. chili powder	1/3 c. milk
15-1/2 oz. can chili beans	1 egg, beaten

Brown ground beef with onion in a skillet over medium heat. Drain; add salt and pepper to taste. Stir in chili powder, beans, tomato sauce and water. Simmer for 5 minutes; remove from heat. Stir together cornbread mix, milk and egg; spoon over beef mixture and place skillet in oven. Bake, uncovered, at 350 degrees for 25 minutes, or until cornbread topping is set and golden. Serves 4 to 6.

Keep the cutting board from slipping while you chop!
Set it on a piece of non-slip mesh easily found at home
improvement stores...it's the same kind of pad
used to keep area rugs from slipping.

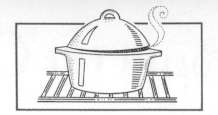

Chicken Pot Pie

Kate Kelly Gallegos
Aurora, IL

My son, Frankie, loves to help make this for dinner.

2 to 3-lb. deli roast chicken, shredded or chopped
10-3/4 oz. can cream of mushroom soup with roasted garlic

16-oz. pkg. frozen mixed vegetables, thawed
2 stalks celery, chopped
12-oz. tube refrigerated dinner rolls

Mix together chicken, soup, vegetables and celery. Spoon into a lightly greased 9"x9" baking pan. Separate and flatten rolls; place on top of mixture. Bake for 25 minutes at 350 degrees, or until bubbly and rolls are golden. Serves 4.

Savory chicken broth...free! After slicing the meat from a deli chicken, cover the bones with water in a stockpot. Onion and celery trimmings can be added too. Simmer gently for 30 to 40 minutes, then strain and refrigerate in recipe-size containers.

Chicken Turnovers

Angela Bettencourt
Mukilteo, WA

This is one of the most requested recipes in our family of five hungry boys...a 13-year-old and four (yes, quadruplets!) 10-year-olds. It is definitely comfort food and we hope everyone who tries it will enjoy it! I double this recipe to feed my hungry crew.

4 c. cooked chicken, cubed
8-oz. pkg. cream cheese,
   softened
1/2 c. milk
1 T. onion, minced
1 t. salt
1/8 t. pepper

2 8-oz. tubes refrigerated
   crescent rolls
1 T. margarine, melted
3/4 c. grated Parmesan cheese
2 10-3/4 oz. cans cream of
   chicken soup
2/3 c. milk

Blend chicken, cream cheese, milk, onion, salt and pepper; set aside. Separate each tube of crescent rolls into 4 rectangles; press to seal perforations. Spoon 1/2 cup chicken mixture into center of each rectangle; pull up corners to form a triangle and press to seal. Place turnovers on an ungreased baking sheet. Brush tops with margarine; sprinkle with Parmesan. Bake, uncovered, at 350 degrees for 20 to 25 minutes, or until golden. While turnovers are baking, combine soup and milk in a saucepan; heat until bubbly. Spoon soup mixture over turnovers. Serves 4 to 6.

Dried, minced onion is handy in all kinds of recipes.
Stir it right into casseroles, or cover with a little
cold water to reconstitute.

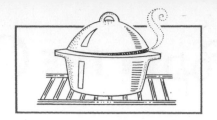

Salsa Chicken

Linda Shively
Hopkinsville, KY

This is so yummy and easy! I make it a complete dinner with instant Mexican rice, diced tomatoes and shredded lettuce.

4 boneless, skinless chicken
  breasts
1 T. plus 3/4 t. taco seasoning
  mix

1 c. mild or hot salsa
1 c. shredded Cheddar cheese
Garnish: sour cream

Place chicken breasts in a lightly greased 13"x9" baking pan. Sprinkle taco seasoning on both sides of chicken; pour salsa over all. Bake, uncovered, at 375 degrees for 25 to 30 minutes, or until chicken is tender and juices run clear. Sprinkle evenly with cheese; bake for an additional 5 minutes, until cheese is melted and bubbly. Dollop with sour cream and serve. Serves 4.

Speedy Chicken Spaghetti

Amanda Mervicker
Austin, TX

For extra zip, use Pepper Jack pasteurized process cheese spread.

16-oz. pkg. spaghetti, cooked
10-oz. can chicken, drained
2 10-3/4 oz. cans cream of
  chicken soup
10-3/4 oz. can cream of
  mushroom soup

10-oz. can diced tomatoes
  with chiles
8-oz. pkg. pasteurized process
  cheese spread, cubed and
  divided

Combine cooked spaghetti, chicken, soups, tomatoes with chiles and 3/4 of cheese; mix well. Place into a greased 3-quart casserole dish; top with remaining cheese. Bake, covered, at 350 degrees for 10 minutes. Uncover and continue to bake for an additional 15 minutes, until bubbly and lightly golden. Makes 6 to 8 servings.

JUST *Pop* IN THE *Oven*

Teeny's Mexican Casserole

Ellen Mattingly
Flagstaff, AZ

*This is a quick recipe that my mother would feed all of us after work.
Growing up in Prescott, Arizona, it was always a treat to eat this once
a week at least. Then after getting married and having 3 children of my
own, I have always had this on our table as well. We lived in New
Orleans for 30 years, but after Hurricane Katrina, we're back in
Arizona again. I hope you all will like it too!*

1 to 1-1/2 lbs. ground beef
1/2 c. onion, chopped
4-oz. can chopped green chiles
3/4 t. salt-free herb seasoning
3/4 t. garlic powder
3/4 t. ground cumin
3/4 t. paprika
salt and pepper to taste

12 6-inch corn tortillas, torn
   into bite-size pieces
10-3/4 oz. can cream of celery
   or mushroom soup
1/4 c. milk
12-oz. pkg. shredded sharp or
   mild Cheddar cheese, divided

Cook ground beef and onion in a skillet until beef is browned and
onion is tender. Drain; stir in chiles and seasonings. Place tortilla
pieces in a large bowl; add soup, milk and 2 cups cheese. Spoon warm
meat mixture over tortillas. Mix all very well and place in a greased
11"x7" baking pan; top with remaining cheese. Bake, uncovered, at
350 degrees for 20 to 25 minutes, until bubbly and golden on top.
Serves 4 to 6.

Some like it hot...but if a dish turns out spicier than you
expected, turn down the heat by stirring in a tablespoon each
of sugar and lemon juice.

Vickie's Enchilada Bake

Vickie

*Serve with wedges of sun-ripened tomato
and sliced avocado...delightful!*

15-oz. can chili with beans
2 10-oz. cans enchilada sauce
2 T. onion, grated
12-oz. pkg. nacho cheese tortilla
　chips, crushed and divided

2-1/2 c. shredded Cheddar
　cheese, divided
1-1/4 c. sour cream

Combine chili, enchilada sauce and onion in a large bowl. Set aside
2 cups crushed chips and 1/2 cup cheese for topping; add remaining
chips and cheese to chili mixture. Spoon mixture into a greased
11"x9" baking pan. Bake, uncovered, at 375 degrees for 20 minutes,
until hot and bubbly. Remove from oven; top with sour cream,
remaining chips and remaining cheese. Return to oven for an
additional 5 minutes, until cheese is melted. Serves 6.

To cover or not to cover? A casserole that's baked uncovered will
have a crisper, more golden topping than one that's covered
during baking...it's your choice.

JUST *Pop* IN THE *Oven*

Chili Rellenos Casserole

Chanelle Rey
Ordway, CO

We love chili rellenos, but stuffing the individual chiles is a lot of fuss.
This yummy recipe goes together in a jiffy!

2 8-oz. cans whole green chiles,
    drained
1 lb. Monterey Jack cheese,
    sliced
6 eggs, beaten

1-1/2 c. all-purpose flour
2 c. milk
3 T. shortening, melted and
    slightly cooled
1/4 t. salt

Layer chiles and cheese slices in a greased 13"x9" baking pan; set aside. Whisk together eggs, flour, milk, shortening and salt; mix well and pour over cheese. Bake, uncovered, at 350 degrees for 30 minutes, or until golden. Serves 6 to 8.

Before covering a cheese-topped dish with aluminum foil, spray the foil with non-stick vegetable spray...the cheese won't stick when it melts.

Twistin' Tilapia

Diane Stout
Zeeland, MI

Cod and haddock are also excellent in this healthful meal-in-one.
Perfect for summer...place packets on a heated grill and cook,
covered, for about 20 minutes.

4 4 to 6-oz. tilapia fillets,
   thawed
2 t. Italian seasoning
1 t. lemon-pepper seasoning
1 t. garlic, minced
1/4 c. butter, sliced

16-oz. pkg. frozen broccoli,
   cauliflower and carrots
16-oz. can diced tomatoes,
   drained
salt and pepper to taste

Place each fish fillet in the center of a separate 12-inch piece of
aluminum foil. Mix seasonings and garlic; sprinkle evenly over fillets.
Top each fillet with butter slices, frozen vegetables and tomatoes.
Sprinkle with salt and pepper to taste. Fold up ends of foil tightly to
create 4 packets; place packets on a baking sheet. Bake at 400 degrees
for 30 minutes, or until fish flakes easily. Serves 4.

For mild, fresh-tasting fish, place frozen fillets in a shallow dish,
cover with milk and let thaw overnight in the fridge.

JUST *Pop* IN THE *Oven*

Salmon Delight

Carol Dreeszen
King Salmon, AK

Here in Alaska we really know our salmon. This is a very simple baked recipe that is out of this world...I guarantee it is delicious!

1-1/2 lb. salmon fillet
2 T. butter, melted
1 c. mayonnaise

14 round buttery crackers, crushed

Pat salmon dry with a paper towel. Spread butter in a 13"x9" baking pan; place salmon in pan skin-side down. Spread mayonnaise over salmon in a thin layer; sprinkle with cracker crumbs until well coated. Bake, uncovered, at 350 degrees for about 20 minutes, or until crumbs turn golden. Slice into serving portions. Serves 4.

Whip up some herbed dill butter to serve with baked or grilled fish. Blend 2 tablespoons softened butter, 2 tablespoons lemon juice, a teaspoon of minced garlic and a teaspoon of dried or fresh dill...heavenly!

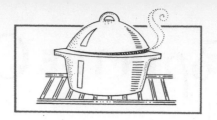

Sloppy Joe Casserole

Leah Shaw
Glasgow, KY

With just four ingredients, this recipe is great when time is short.

1 lb. ground beef
16-oz. can Sloppy Joe sauce
2 8-oz. tubes refrigerated
   crescent rolls

8-oz. pkg. shredded Cheddar
   cheese

Brown ground beef in a skillet; drain. Stir in sauce. Unroll one tube of crescent rolls; spread out in the bottom of a 13"x9" baking pan that has been sprayed with non-stick vegetable spray. Top rolls with meat mixture; sprinkle with cheese. Add second can of crescent rolls on top and smooth out. Bake, uncovered, at 350 degrees for 20 to 30 minutes, until golden. Serves 6.

Cheese tends to turn crumbly when frozen...not so good for a recipe using fresh cheese, but perfectly fine in baked casserole dishes. Go ahead and stock up when cheese is on sale...just thaw overnight in the refrigerator before using.

Jax's Cheeseburger Pizza

Jackie Daunce
Lockport, NY

This is a fast and easy supper I whip up for my husband and two boys. There are never any leftovers!

1 lb. ground turkey
1/2 c. onion, diced
1/2 t. garlic salt
1/2 t. pepper
2 12-inch Italian pizza crusts

catsup and mustard to taste
16-oz. jar sliced bread & butter
  pickles, drained
8-oz. pkg. shredded Cheddar
  cheese

In a skillet over medium heat, brown turkey and onion; sprinkle with garlic salt and pepper. Drain and set aside. Place pizza crusts on ungreased baking sheets. Swirl catsup onto crusts, as you would do on a hamburger bun. Swirl mustard on top of the catsup (no need to smooth out or mix together). Divide turkey mixture evenly between the 2 crusts; arrange pickles on top of turkey. Sprinkle evenly with cheese. Bake at 425 degrees for 12 to 15 minutes, until cheese has melted. Cut into wedges to serve. Makes 2 pizzas, 8 servings each.

For a crisp pizzeria-style finish, dust the pizza pan
with cornmeal before adding the crust.

Layered Mexican Pizzas

Helene Gibson
Yuma, AZ

Double-decker delights made with crisp tostada shells.

1 lb. ground beef
1-1/4 oz. pkg. burrito
  seasoning mix
12 corn tostada shells
16-oz. can refried beans
8-oz. pkg. shredded Mexican-
  blend cheese

10-oz. can red enchilada sauce
2 c. shredded lettuce
14-1/2 oz. can diced tomatoes
  with chiles
1 onion, chopped

Brown ground beef in a skillet over medium heat. Drain; add
seasoning mix according to package directions. You will use 2 shells
for each pizza. Spread 6 shells with refried beans. Layer ground beef
mixture over refried beans; top with cheese and one tablespoon sauce
per shell. Place remaining shells on top; sprinkle with lettuce,
tomatoes with chiles and onion. Cover with cheese and drizzle with
one tablespoon sauce per shell. Place on a lightly greased baking
sheet. Bake at 350 degrees for about 5 minutes, just until cheese
melts. Makes 6 servings.

Canned diced tomatoes with the seasonings included are
wonderful for creating speedy suppers. With flavorful extras like
roasted garlic, basil, sweet onions or even green chiles, there are
fewer ingredients for you to buy and measure.

Becky's Ground Beef Casserole
Stephanie Buchholtz
Toledo, OH

When I was a kid, we went to visit our cousins in Paris, Illinois and my cousin, Becky, made this for us one night. My sister and I were fussy kids, so when we gobbled it up, my mom just had to ask for the recipe! Now I serve it to my family and they love it too.

1 lb. ground beef
1 onion, chopped
8-oz. pkg. medium egg noodles,
   cooked
10-3/4 oz. can cream of
   chicken soup

10-3/4 oz. cream of
   mushroom soup
8-oz. container sour cream
1/2 c. butter, melted
1 sleeve saltine crackers,
   crushed

In a skillet over medium heat, brown beef and onion together; drain. Combine beef mixture, cooked noodles, soups and sour cream; place in a greased 13"x9" baking pan. Combine butter and crushed crackers; mix well and sprinkle over top of casserole. Bake, uncovered, at 350 degrees for 30 minutes. Serves 8.

It's so easy to double casserole recipes and freeze half for another night! Just remember...add only 1-1/2 times the amount of salt originally called for, then taste and adjust.

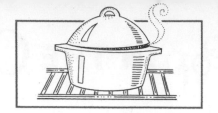

Chicken Oregano

Julie Bruninga
Edwardsville, IL

Serve over thin spaghetti...pass the Parmesan cheese, please!

1-1/2 lbs. boneless, skinless
   chicken breasts
15-oz. can tomato sauce
28-oz. can diced tomatoes
1 green pepper, thinly sliced
1 onion, thinly sliced

1 t. garlic salt
1 t. dried oregano
salt and pepper to taste
1/2 c. shredded mozzarella
   cheese

Place chicken in a lightly greased 13"x9" baking pan. Top with sauce and tomatoes. Arrange green pepper and onion on top; sprinkle with seasonings and cheese. Bake, uncovered, at 375 degrees for 30 minutes, until chicken juices run clear. Serves 4.

Zesty Ranch Chicken

Beth Bundy
Long Prairie, MN

After a busy day, it takes just a few minutes to slide this dish into the oven. Relax...dinner will be ready soon!

1/2 c. ranch salad dressing
1 T. all-purpose flour
4 boneless, skinless chicken
   breasts

1/4 c. shredded Cheddar cheese

Mix together salad dressing and flour. Coat chicken in mixture; arrange in a lightly greased 8"x8" baking pan. Top with cheese. Bake, uncovered, at 350 degrees for 25 minutes, until chicken juices run clear. Serves 4.

Lay a piece of wax paper on the counter before crumb-coating meat... when you're finished, just fold up the paper and toss away the mess!

Mushroom-Garlic Chicken Pizza

Judy Davis
Muskogee, OK

*This recipe gets a big "YUM" at our house...try it! It's a great way
to use leftover baked or grilled chicken too.*

12-inch Italian pizza crust
3/4 c. ranch salad dressing
2 T. garlic, minced
1 chicken breast, cooked and
  sliced

2 4-oz. cans sliced mushrooms,
  drained
salt and pepper to taste
8-oz. pkg. shredded mozzarella
  cheese

Place crust on an ungreased pizza pan or baking sheet. Spread salad
dressing and garlic on crust. Arrange sliced chicken and mushrooms
on top. Add salt and pepper to taste; cover with cheese. Bake at
400 degrees until cheese is melted, about 8 to 10 minutes. Cut into
wedges. Makes 6 to 8 servings.

For juicy, tender chicken in recipes calling for cooked chicken,
try poaching. Cover boneless, skinless chicken breasts with
water in a saucepan. Bring to a boil, then turn down the heat,
cover and simmer over low heat for 10 to 12 minutes.
The chicken is done when it is no longer pink in the center.

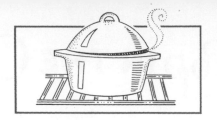

Loaded Potato Casserole

Trisha Klempel
Sidney, MT

One night I needed to pull together a last-minute supper from the ingredients I had on hand. We were all pleasantly surprised by how yummy this turned out! Now it's a family favorite.

1 lb. ground beef
1/2 lb. bacon, chopped
4.9-oz. pkg. au gratin potato mix
2 c. boiling water
1 c. half-and-half
8-oz. pkg. shredded Colby
   Jack cheese

1/4 c. green onion, chopped
pepper and dried parsley to taste
Optional: 1/2 c. bread crumbs,
   1 to 2 T. melted butter, onion
   salt and dried parsley to taste

Brown beef and bacon together in a skillet over medium heat. Drain; set aside. Stir together potato mix with seasoning packet, water, half-and-half, cheese, onion, pepper and parsley in a lightly greased 2-1/2 quart casserole dish; stir in meat mixture. Bake, uncovered, at 375 degrees for 30 minutes. If desired, make a topping by mixing together optional ingredients; sprinkle over casserole during last 10 minutes of baking. Serves 6.

Try crushed tortilla chips as a crunchy casserole topping.
They come in so many flavors like white corn, Cheddar
cheese, ranch and spicy chili...there's sure to be one
that's a hit with your family!

Macaroni & Cheese Deluxe

Lanita Anderson
Chesapeake, VA

So good, it melts in your mouth!

8-oz. pkg. elbow macaroni,
  uncooked
2 c. cream-style cottage cheese
1 c. sour cream
1 egg, beaten
3/4 t. salt

1/2 t. pepper
1/2 t. garlic powder
8-oz. pkg. shredded Cheddar
  cheese
Optional: paprika to taste

Measure out 1-1/2 cups macaroni, reserving the rest for another
recipe. Cook macaroni according to package directions; drain and set
aside. Combine cottage cheese, sour cream, egg and seasonings. Add
Cheddar cheese and mix well; add cooked macaroni and stir until
coated. Transfer to a greased 13"x9" baking pan. Bake, uncovered,
at 350 degrees for 25 to 30 minutes, or until heated through. Sprinkle
with paprika, if desired. Makes 6 to 8 servings.

If you love macaroni & cheese with a chewy, crusty topping,
but hate to scrub the baked-on cheese in the casserole dish
afterwards, try this! Fill the dish with warm water and add
a teaspoon or two of baking soda. Let stand overnight.
The next day, the baked-on portion will loosen easily.

Katie's Taco Casserole

Katie Cooper
Chubbuck, ID

Garnish with all your favorite taco toppings like sour cream, shredded lettuce, diced tomatoes and sliced black olives.

1 lb. ground beef
1 t. dried, minced onion
1/2 c. frozen corn
2 8-oz. cans tomato sauce
2 t. chili powder
7-oz. pkg. tortilla chips

10-3/4 oz. can cream of
  chicken soup
3/4 c. milk
1 c. shredded Mexican-blend
  cheese

Brown ground beef in a skillet over medium heat; drain. Add onion, corn, tomato sauce and chili powder; simmer for one minute. Arrange enough tortilla chips to cover the bottom of a lightly greased 13"x9" baking pan; press down lightly to crush chips coarsely. Spoon beef mixture over chips. Mix soup and milk; spoon over top. Sprinkle with cheese. Bake, uncovered, at 350 degrees for 30 minutes. Serve with remaining tortilla chips. Makes 6 servings.

Stock up on canned goods like diced tomatoes, corn, beans, tomato sauce and cream soups whenever they go on sale. Add some ground beef or chicken, and you'll be able to stir up all kinds of family-friendly casseroles in a jiffy.

Speedy Burritos

Mariarosa De Marco-Fleming
Elyria, OH

With this recipe I can feed my husband and my three kids quickly on a busy night! It's very flexible...depending on what I have on hand, I will add corn and sliced olives to the skillet along with the refried beans or even use shredded chicken instead of beef.

1 lb. ground beef
1-1/4 oz. pkg. taco seasoning
   mix
3/4 c. water
2 16-oz. cans refried beans
8-oz. pkg. cream cheese,
   softened and cubed

8 burrito-size flour tortillas
24-oz. pkg. shredded Mexican-
   blend cheese
garnish: sour cream

Brown beef in a skillet over medium heat; drain. Add seasoning and water; heat through. Stir in beans and cream cheese; heat through. Spray a 13"x9" glass baking pan with non-stick vegetable spray; set aside. Spoon 1/8 of meat mixture onto a tortilla; roll up and place seam-side down in pan. Repeat with remaining tortillas, fitting into pan. Top with cheese. Bake, uncovered, at 350 degrees for 10 to 15 minutes, until cheese melts. Serve topped with dollops of sour cream. Makes 8 servings.

Fix a double batch! Brown two pounds of ground beef with two packages of taco seasoning mix, then freeze half of the mixture for a quick meal of tacos or taco salad another night.

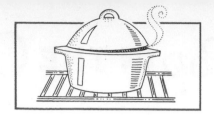

Mary's Meatballs

Mary Novotny
Ironton, MN

All four of our kids love these meatballs!

1-1/2 lbs. ground beef
1 onion, chopped
1/4 c. catsup
1 T. Worcestershire sauce
1 t. mustard

1 egg, beaten
1/2 to 3/4 c. Italian-flavored
   dry bread crumbs
Optional: barbecue sauce

Mix all ingredients except barbecue sauce in a large bowl. Shape into 2-inch balls and place on greased baking sheets. Bake at 350 degrees for about 30 minutes, or until browned and internal temperature reads 170 degrees with a meat thermometer. If desired, drizzle with barbecue sauce before serving. Serves 4 to 6.

Dip your hands into cold water before shaping meatballs...
the meat won't stick to your hands.

Cabbage Crescent Rolls

Lana Rulevish
Ashley, IL

I have had this recipe for years. It's much quicker to fix than traditional cabbage rolls with the beef mixture rolled up in cabbage leaves. Many of my guests have said they like it better too!

1 lb. lean ground beef
1 head cabbage, finely chopped
1/4 c. water
1/8 t. garlic salt
salt and pepper to taste

8-oz. tube refrigerated crescent rolls
Optional: melted butter
1 c. shredded Cheddar cheese

In a large skillet over medium heat, brown beef; drain. Add cabbage, water and seasonings; stir thoroughly. Cover and simmer for about 15 minutes. Press crescent rolls together in pairs to form rectangles; place on a lightly greased baking sheet. Spoon meat mixture onto rolls. Fold 2 opposite corners to the center; use a fork to crimp edges and pierce top. Bake at 350 degrees for 10 minutes, or until golden. Remove from oven; brush tops with butter, if desired. Sprinkle with cheese; serve immediately. Makes 4 servings.

Keep a tube or two of refrigerated crescent rolls on hand for quick-to-fix meals! Top dough with tomato sauce and cheese for a speedy pizza, use it to cover a chicken pot pie or even sprinkle with cinnamon-sugar and bake for a sweet treat to enjoy with after-dinner coffee.

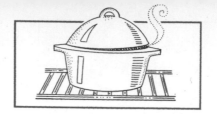

Kimberly's Taquito Bake

Kimberly Wigley
Chesterton, IN

So yummy and it couldn't be easier...it takes me back to Texas every time I make it! Try Mexican-style shredded cheese for added zest.

22-1/2 oz. pkg. frozen flour
   chicken & cheese taquitos
10-3/4 oz. can cream of
   mushroom soup
10-oz. can green enchilada
   sauce

10-oz. can diced tomatoes
   with chiles
8-oz. pkg. shredded Colby
   Jack cheese
Garnish: sour cream, salsa,
   tortilla chips

Arrange frozen taquitos in a single layer in a 13"x9" baking pan sprayed with non-stick vegetable spray; set aside. Mix together soup, sauce and tomatoes with chiles; spoon mixture over taquitos. Bake, uncovered, at 350 degrees for 25 to 30 minutes, until cheese melts. Serve garnished with sour cream, salsa and tortilla chips on the side. Serves 8 to 10.

Spice a dish with love and it pleases
every palate.
-Plautus

JUST *Pop* IN THE *Oven*

Cheesy Corn & Bean Burritos

Angela Leikem
Silverton, OR

Fresh cilantro kicks up the flavor of common pantry staples.

15-oz. can black beans, drained
  and rinsed
16-oz. can corn, drained
8-oz. can chopped green chiles,
  drained
12-oz. pkg. shredded Monterey
  Jack cheese, divided

1 bunch fresh cilantro, divided
2 c. cooked rice
6 to 8 10-inch flour tortillas
16-oz. jar salsa, divided

Combine beans, corn, chiles, 2 cups cheese and 1/2 bunch chopped cilantro; stir in cooked rice. Spoon 1/2 cup bean mixture along the center of each tortilla; top with 2 tablespoons salsa. Roll up burrito-style and arrange seam-side down in a greased 13"x9" baking pan. Spread any remaining bean mixture over burritos. Spoon remaining salsa over burritos and into corners of pan; top with remaining cheese. Cover loosely with aluminum foil. Bake at 425 degrees for 30 minutes, until heated through and cheese has melted. Garnish with remaining cilantro, as desired. Serves 6 to 8.

Keep kitchen sponges smelling lemony fresh! Soak them in lemon juice, then rinse well with clear water.

Honey Chicken & Stuffing

Angela Murphy
Tempe, AZ

*An all-in-one family meal that's good enough for guests! Best of all,
it's easy to make ahead...prepare, tuck in the fridge and then bake
just in time for dinner.*

3 c. herb-flavored stuffing mix
1 c. hot water
1/2 c. golden raisins
2 T. butter, melted
6 boneless, skinless chicken
   breasts

1/2 c. honey
1/3 c. mayonnaise
1/3 c. Dijon mustard
1/2 t. dried parsley

Combine stuffing, water, raisins and butter; toss to mix and let
stand for 3 minutes. Spoon stuffing mixture in 6 mounds into a
13"x9" baking pan sprayed with non-stick vegetable spray. Place
one chicken breast on top of each mound. Mix together remaining
ingredients; spoon over chicken. Cover baking pan with aluminum
foil. Bake at 400 degrees for 25 to 30 minutes. Remove foil and bake
for an additional 5 minutes, until golden. Serves 6.

When measuring sticky ingredients like honey, peanut butter or
molasses, spray the measuring cup with non-stick vegetable
spray first. The contents will slip right out and you'll get
a more accurate measurement.

JUST *Pop* IN THE *Oven*

Easy Garlic-Parmesan Chicken

Denise Allison
Gig Harbor, WA

My handy tip...for easy clean-up, line the pan with aluminum foil before spraying it with non-stick vegetable spray.

3/4 c. mayonnaise
1/2 c. grated Parmesan cheese
1 t. garlic powder
1 t. Italian seasoning

4 to 6 boneless, skinless
 chicken breasts
1 c. Italian-flavored dry bread
 crumbs

Mix mayonnaise, cheese and seasonings in a shallow bowl. Coat chicken breasts with mixture; cover with bread crumbs. Arrange in a 13"x9" baking pan that has been sprayed with non-stick vegetable spray. Bake, uncovered, at 425 degrees for 20 to 25 minutes, until golden and chicken juices run clear. Serves 4 to 6.

For a healthy change, give whole-wheat pasta a try in your favorite pasta recipe...it tastes great and contains more fiber than regular pasta.

Easy Turkey Noodle Bake

Joanne Callahan
Far Hills, NJ

I like to roast turkeys year 'round as the scent and taste bring back such sweet memories of the Thanksgivings of my childhood. This casserole is a quick, satisfying use for all those leftovers.

8-oz. pkg. egg noodles,
    uncooked and divided
2 c. cooked turkey, cut into
    bite-size pieces

12-oz. jar turkey gravy
1 t. dried sage
2 t. onion powder
1 c. frozen corn, thawed

Measure out 2 cups noodles, reserving the rest for another recipe. Cook noodles according to package directions; drain. Combine with remaining ingredients in a large bowl; mix thoroughly. If mixture seems too dry, add a small amount of water. Spoon into a lightly greased 9"x9" baking pan. Cover and bake at 350 degrees for 30 minutes, until heated through. Serves 4.

Keep some festive paper plates and napkins tucked away...
they'll set a lighthearted mood on busy evenings,
with easy clean-up afterwards.

JUST *Pop* IN THE *Oven*

Cheesy Beefy Squash Casserole

Julie Pak
Henryetta, OK

This recipe is such a big hit with my family during the summer, when we are harvesting lots of fresh squash from the garden.

2 lbs. yellow squash, cut into
   3/4-inch cubes
1 T. oil
1 lb. ground beef
1 onion, chopped
1 T. garlic salt

1 c. long-cooking rice, uncooked
16-oz. container cottage cheese
2 10-3/4 oz. cans cream of
   mushroom soup
1-1/4 c. milk
1 c. shredded Cheddar cheese

In a skillet over medium heat, sauté squash in oil until crisp-tender. In a separate skillet, brown ground beef with onion and garlic salt; drain. Stir uncooked rice into beef mixture. In a 13"x9" baking pan sprayed with non-stick vegetable spray, layer half of beef mixture, half of squash, remaining beef mixture, cottage cheese and remaining squash. Mix soup and milk in a microwave-safe bowl; microwave for one minute on high and pour over casserole. Bake, uncovered, at 350 degrees for 25 minutes. Sprinkle cheese on top and bake until cheese melts, about 5 minutes. Serves 6.

Handy gadgets like mini choppers make prep work a breeze
for chopping potatoes, onions, tomatoes or peppers...
what a time-saver!

Chicken Pizza Pizazz

Beth Flack
Terre Haute, IN

*Pick up a loaf of crusty French bread and turn leftover chicken
into a fresh and tasty dinner.*

1 loaf French bread, halved
   lengthwise
8-oz. can pizza sauce
1 c. cooked chicken, diced
1 c. zucchini, quartered and
   sliced

1/4 lb. pasteurized process
   cheese spread, cubed
1/3 c. sliced black olives
1 t. Italian seasoning

Place both halves of loaf on an ungreased baking sheet, cut-side up.
Combine remaining ingredients; mix lightly. Spread each bread half
with half of mixture; cover with aluminum foil. Bake at 350 degrees
for 25 to 30 minutes, or until cheese is melted. Slice to serve. Makes
6 to 8 servings.

French Bread Sausage Pizza

Christine Gordon
Rapid City, SD

*A quick & easy dinner...kids will love to eat this as much as they love
helping Mom make it! Change it up any way you like, adding other
pizza toppings to your own taste.*

1 loaf French bread, halved
   lengthwise
15-oz. can pizza sauce
1 lb. ground pork sausage,
   browned and drained

3-1/2 oz. pkg. sliced pepperoni
8-oz. pkg. shredded mozzarella
   cheese

Place both halves of loaf on an ungreased baking sheet, cut-side up.
Spread with pizza sauce; top with sausage, pepperoni and cheese.
Bake at 350 degrees for 15 minutes, or until cheese is melted. Slice
to serve. Makes 6 to 8 servings.

SIMMERING Soup Pots

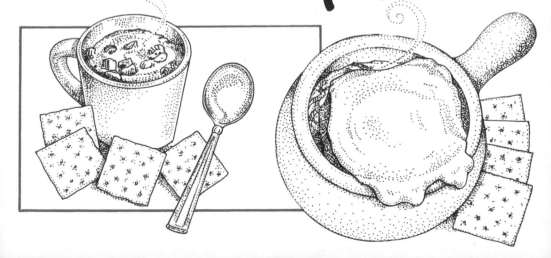

Italian Sausage Soup

Deb Quillen
Creston, OH

A friend told me about a soup she had really enjoyed. I took her description and made this soup...she says it's even better than she remembers!

2 lbs. Italian turkey sausages,
   casings removed
1 onion, chopped
3 qts. chicken broth
4 potatoes, peeled and cubed
10-oz. pkg. frozen chopped
   spinach

2 c. half-and-half
1 c. grated Parmesan cheese
Garnish: additional grated
   Parmesan cheese

Brown sausages and onion in a large Dutch oven over medium heat; drain. Add broth and potatoes; simmer until potatoes are tender, about 15 minutes. Add frozen spinach and half-and-half; continue simmering until hot. Just before serving, stir in Parmesan cheese; serve sprinkled with extra cheese. Serves 6.

A soup supper is warm and comforting on a chilly night... it's so easy to prepare too. Just add a basket of muffins and a crock of sweet butter...dinner is served!

SIMMERING Soup Pots

Speedy Meatball Soup

Juliet Makarewicz
Alamogordo, NM

Tomatoes packed with chiles give this soup a zesty flavor, but you can use any seasoned diced tomatoes that you prefer.

14-1/2 oz. can chicken or
   beef broth
2 c. water
12-oz. pkg. frozen meatballs
16-oz. pkg. frozen stir-fry or
   other mixed vegetables

14-1/2 oz. can diced tomatoes
   with chiles
1/4 c. small soup pasta,
   uncooked

Combine all ingredients together in a large saucepan. Simmer over medium heat until all ingredients are tender, about 10 to 15 minutes. Serves 4.

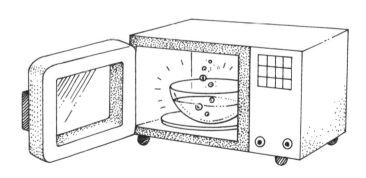

Get soup off to a speedy start! Bring the water or broth to a boil in the microwave while you're assembling the other ingredients.

BBQ Sloppy Joe Soup

Betty Lou Wright
Hendersonville, TN

This recipe was a happy accident! One day I made vegetable soup, then realized I had some leftover Sloppy Joe meat sauce in the fridge. To use it up, I added the Sloppy Joe sauce to the soup. What a hit! It's a great stick-to-the-ribs soup for those chilly winter days.

1 lb. ground beef chuck
16-oz. can barbecue Sloppy Joe sauce
10-3/4 oz. can cream of potato soup
10-3/4 oz. can minestrone soup
1-1/4 c. water
15-oz. can light red kidney beans, drained and rinsed

14-1/2 oz. can green beans, drained
15-1/4 oz. can green peas, drained
15-oz. can diced tomatoes, drained
garlic powder and steak seasoning powder to taste
Garnish: oyster crackers

In a large saucepan over medium heat, brown ground beef; drain. Stir in Sloppy Joe sauce; heat through. Add remaining ingredients except crackers and simmer until bubbly, about 10 to 15 minutes. Serve with oyster crackers. Makes 6 to 8 servings.

Save the water that vegetables have been cooked in...it makes a flavorful addition to your next pot of soup.

SIMMERING Soup Pots

Nana's Country Chili

Eva Drummond
Timberville, VA

This is a recipe that I make a lot when we go camping. It is so easy to prepare! My hubby likes it a little thinner so he can put crackers in it... just add some tomato juice or water while it's simmering.

2 lbs. ground beef
1 onion, chopped
2 28-oz. cans tomato sauce
2 49-oz. cans kidney beans,
   drained and rinsed

24-oz. jar mild salsa
2 1-1/4 oz. pkgs. chili
   seasoning mix

Brown ground beef in a large heavy stockpot over medium heat. Add onion and cook until translucent. Drain; stir in remaining ingredients. Bring to a boil, stirring frequently. Reduce heat; simmer for about 30 minutes, stirring frequently. Makes 8 to 10 servings.

There's no such thing as too much chili! Freeze leftovers in small containers, to be microwaved and spooned over hot dogs or baked potatoes.

Fishermen's Stew

*Kathleen Dolge
Jacksonville, FL*

*This flavorful chowder can be put together in a flash!
Garnish with fish-shaped crackers just for fun.*

2 t. olive oil
2 c. turkey Kielbasa, diced
2 onions, chopped
4 c. chicken broth
8-oz. bottle clam juice
2 6-oz. cans chopped clams
3/4 to 1 lb. cod or halibut, cut
   into 1-inch cubes

15-oz. can chickpeas, drained
   and rinsed
1 sweet potato, peeled and
   cubed
1 bay leaf
2 t. lemon juice
1/4 t. pepper

Heat oil in a large saucepan. Add Kielbasa and onions; stir until onions soften. Stir in broth, clam juice, clams with juice, fish, chickpeas, sweet potato and bay leaf. Simmer until fish is opaque and sweet potato is tender, about 10 minutes. Before serving, discard bay leaf; stir in lemon juice and pepper. Makes 4 to 6 servings.

A quick trick to fix watery soup...thicken it with just a sprinkling of instant potato flakes.

Simple Seafood Chowder

Carol Blessing
Averill Park, NY

This is my most requested recipe! It's a perfect comfort food...I am comforted knowing that it turns out perfectly every time I make it, and its rich, hearty and satisfying flavor says "welcome" to every guest. Serve with a lovely warm crusty bread.

1/4 c. butter
1 stalk celery, diced
1/4 t. dried thyme
1/4 t. pepper
3 T. biscuit baking mix
15-oz. can lobster bisque
2. 10-3/4 oz. cans cream of
   potato soup

3-1/2 c. milk
1-1/2 lbs. seafood like shrimp,
   scallops and crab, peeled
   or cleaned and cut into
   bite-size pieces
3 to 4 green onions, thinly
   sliced

Melt butter in a large heavy saucepan over low heat; sauté celery until tender. Stir in seasonings and baking mix. Add bisque, soup and milk; cook and stir until smooth. Increase heat to medium. When soup is hot, add seafood. Stir occasionally. Add green onions about 5 minutes after adding seafood: Heat until seafood is cooked through. Serves 6.

Keep a few cans of evaporated milk in the pantry for extra creamy-tasting soups. Evaporated milk can be substituted whenever a recipe calls for regular milk.

Tomato & Spinach Soup

Joely Flegler
Tulsa, OK

Delicious and oh-so-easy to stir up! For a bisque-style soup,
drizzle in some cream after removing from the heat.

2 cloves garlic, minced
2 T. olive oil
14-1/2 oz. can stewed tomatoes

14-1/2 oz. can diced tomatoes
1 to 2 c. baby spinach

In a saucepan over medium heat, sauté garlic in oil until tender. Stir in both undrained cans of tomatoes. Cook on medium-low heat until warmed through. Add spinach; cook and stir until spinach is slightly wilted. Serves 4 to 6.

To mellow the flavor of tomato soup,
stir in a teaspoon of sugar.

SIMMERING Soup Pots

Hearty Veggie Soup

Shawna Sylvester
Saint Paul, MN

This is a great basic soup recipe using ingredients from the pantry.
Add your own touches...my husband added leftover grilled chicken
and some crushed tortilla chips and it was even better!

4 c. chicken broth
15-oz. can light kidney beans,
   drained and rinsed
15-oz. can dark kidney beans,
   drained and rinsed

2 15-oz. cans diced tomatoes
2 15-oz. cans mixed vegetables,
   drained
3 T. dried, minced onion

Mix all ingredients together in a large soup pot. Cook over medium-low heat until heated through, about 15 minutes. Serves 8.

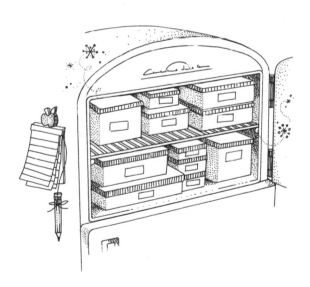

Keep a container in your freezer for leftover veggies. Whenever you are ready to make soup or stew, just toss them in...so thrifty!

Mexican Corn Soup

Laura Justice
Indianapolis, IN

*Your family will love this filling soup...it warms you right up
on a rainy day!*

3 10-3/4 oz. cans cream of
  chicken soup
14-oz. can chicken broth
10-oz. can diced tomatoes
  with chiles
1 clove garlic, minced

1/4 t. pepper
3 8-oz. pkgs. pasteurized
  process cheese spread, cubed
16-oz. pkg. frozen corn
2 c. cooked chicken, chopped

In a soup pot over medium heat, combine soup, broth, tomatoes with
chiles, garlic and pepper; bring to a simmer. Add cheese and stir until
melted, creamy and smooth. Stir in corn and chicken; simmer for
about 20 minutes. Serves 8.

Crunchy toppings can really add fun and flavor to soup or chili.
Some fun choices...fish-shaped crackers, bacon bits, French fried
onions, sunflower seeds or toasted nuts. Yummy!

SIMMERING *Soup Pots*

Lisa's Chicken Tortilla Soup

Lisa Johnson
Hallsville, TX

*I've tossed this soup together on many occasions. It's a snap to make...
a real life-saver when extra people turn up for supper!*

4 14-1/2 oz. cans chicken broth
4 10-oz. cans diced tomatoes
  with chiles
1 c. canned or frozen corn
30-oz. can refried beans

5 c. cooked chicken, shredded
Garnish: shredded Mexican-
  blend or Monterey Jack
  cheese, corn chips or
  tortilla strips

In a large stockpot over medium heat, combine broth and tomatoes
with chiles. Stir in corn and beans; bring to a boil. Reduce heat to low
and simmer for 5 minutes, stirring frequently. Add chicken and heat
through. Top off bowls of soup with shredded cheese and corn chips
or tortilla strips. Makes 6 to 8 servings.

Canned yellow or white hominy makes a tasty, filling addition
to any southwestern-style soup.

Dad's Chicken Stew

Cynthia Bullington
Rancho Cucamonga, CA

My dad takes care of my mom and does all the cooking. He especially loves to make stew. This is my all-time favorite "comfort food" recipe that he has handed down to me.

1/3 c. all-purpose flour
1/2 t. salt
1/4 t. pepper
3 boneless, skinless chicken
   breasts, cut into 1-inch cubes
3 T. olive oil
1 onion, sliced
3 celery stalks, sliced

3 carrots, peeled and sliced
2 potatoes, peeled and cut into
   3/4-inch cubes
1 c. chicken broth
1/2 t. dried thyme
1 T. catsup
1 T. cornstarch

Combine flour, salt and pepper; coat chicken. In a large skillet over medium heat, brown chicken in oil. Add onion and celery; cook for 3 minutes. Stir in carrots and potatoes. Combine remaining ingredients; stir into skillet. Bring to a boil. Reduce heat; cover and simmer for 15 to 20 minutes, or until vegetables are tender. Serves 4 to 6.

Top a bubbling stew with big, fluffy dumplings...it's easy!
Cut refrigerated buttermilk biscuits into quarters and drop
into simmering stew or soup. Continue simmering
for 10 to 15 minutes, until done.

SIMMERING Soup Pots

Chris's Vegetable Beef Soup

Christina Mendoza
Alamogordo, NM

*It was cold outside and we were hungry for vegetable beef soup, so
I came up with this one. It was very good! I served it with saltines
and hot garlic dill pickles on the side...scrumptious!*

1 lb. ground beef
1 onion, chopped
2 to 4 stalks celery, chopped
3 T. olive oil
15-oz. can diced tomatoes
14-1/2 oz. can diced potatoes,
　 drained

1 clove garlic, pressed
14-oz. pkg. frozen mixed
　 vegetables
5 c. beef broth
Optional: 1 c. bowtie pasta,
　 uncooked

Place ground beef, onion, celery and oil in a Dutch oven; brown well
over medium heat. Drain; add remaining ingredients. Simmer over
medium heat until vegetables are tender, about 10 minutes. Makes
about 8 servings.

A delicious way to use leftover roast beef...chop or shred and use
instead of ground beef in your favorite soup recipe.

Easy Cabbage Stew

Teresa Stiegelmeyer
Indianapolis, IN

In a hurry? Pick up a bag of coleslaw mix...no need to shred cabbage.

1 head cabbage, shredded
1 lb. smoked sausage, sliced
10-3/4 oz. can cream of celery
    soup

salt and pepper to taste

Place cabbage and sausage in a large soup pot; add just enough water to cover. Simmer over medium heat for about 20 minutes, until cabbage is tender. Do not drain. Stir in soup, salt and pepper; heat through. Makes 4 to 6 servings.

A dash of cider vinegar adds zing to any cabbage dish.

Golden Cream Soup

Loyce Wright
Pampa, TX

My whole family just loves this creamy and comforting soup.

3 c. potatoes, peeled and
   chopped
1/2 c. celery, sliced
1/2 c. carrots, peeled and sliced
1/4 c. onion, chopped
1 c. water
1 t. chicken bouillon granules

1 t. dried parsley
1/2 t. salt
1/8 t. pepper
2 T. all-purpose flour
1-1/2 c. milk
8-oz. pkg. pasteurized process
   cheese spread, cubed

In a large saucepan, combine vegetables, water, bouillon and
seasonings; mix well. Cover; simmer over medium heat for
15 minutes, or until vegetables are tender. Place flour in a medium
bowl. Gradually add milk, whisking until well blended. Add mixture
to soup; cook and stir until thickened. Add cheese; stir until melted.
Serves 6.

Crisp, savory crackers are delightful alongside a steamy bowl
of soup. Spread saltines with softened butter and sprinkle
with Italian seasoning and garlic powder. Bake at 350 degrees
for just a few minutes, until golden.

Cheesy Chicken Chowder

Sally Schellenberger
Pittsburgh, PA

I have served this chowder often to company
and they always request the recipe.

2 14-1/2 oz. cans chicken broth
2 c. potatoes, peeled and diced
1 c. carrots, peeled and sliced
1 c. onion, diced
1 t. pepper
1/4 c. butter

1/3 c. all-purpose flour
2 c. milk
2 c. pasteurized process cheese
   spread, cubed
2 c. cooked chicken, diced

Combine broth, vegetables and pepper in a large saucepan. Bring
to a boil over medium heat. Reduce heat; cover and simmer for
15 minutes, until vegetables are tender. In a separate saucepan, melt
butter over medium heat; add flour and mix well. Stir in milk; cook
and stir until thickened. Add cheese and stir until melted; stir cheese
mixture into soup. Stir in chicken; heat through. Serves 6.

Need a quick after-school snack to tide the kids over until
dinnertime? Hand out little bags of crunchy snacks...just toss
together bite-size cereal squares, raisins or dried cranberries
and a few chocolate-covered candies.

SIMMERING Soup Pots

Easy Potato-Cheddar Soup

Sara Downing
Whitehall, OH

I keep all of the ingredients for this soup in my pantry...it can be tossed together in 15 minutes!

10-3/4 oz. can cream of potato soup
10-3/4 oz. can Cheddar cheese soup
3 c. milk

1/4 t. salt
1/8 t. pepper
2 16-oz. cans whole potatoes, drained and diced

Combine soups, milk, salt and pepper in a large soup pot over medium heat; stir until blended. Add potatoes; simmer until hot and bubbly. Serves 6.

I live on good soup, not on fine words.
-Moliere

Tortellini-Spinach Soup

Lois Valeri
Sicklerville, NJ

Sprinkle with freshly shredded Parmesan cheese...delicious!

2 cloves garlic, minced
1 T. olive oil
2 14-1/2 oz. cans chicken broth
14-1/2 oz. can stewed tomatoes
9-oz. pkg. cheese tortellini,
   uncooked

10-oz. pkg. frozen chopped
   spinach, thawed and drained
salt and pepper to taste

In a large soup pot over medium-high heat, sauté garlic in oil for
2 to 3 minutes. Add broth and tomatoes with juice; turn heat up to
high and bring to a boil. Stir in tortellini and cook according to
package instructions. When tortellini is almost done, add spinach;
heat through. Add salt and pepper to taste. Makes 6 servings.

Slice onions from the top down, cutting into the root end last...
no more tears! An extra-sharp knife is helpful too.

SIMMERING *Soup Pots*

Aunt Joan's Broccoli-Cheese Soup
Krysti Hilfiger
Covington, PA

When I was young, I loved this soup so much that my aunt always had it bubbling on the stove when I came to stay. It's still oh-so satisfying!

1/2 c. water
10-oz. pkg. frozen chopped
   broccoli
1 T. onion, minced
10-3/4 oz. can cream of
   chicken soup

1 c. milk
1 c. shredded Cheddar cheese
1/8 t. pepper

In a medium saucepan over medium heat, bring water to a boil. Add broccoli and onion. Cover and simmer for 5 minutes, or until broccoli is tender; do not drain. Stir in soup, milk, cheese and pepper. Cook and stir about 4 minutes, or until heated through. Serves 4.

For thick, creamy vegetable soup, use a hand-held immersion
blender to purée some of the cooked veggies
right in the saucepan.

A-to-Z Soup

Nancy Girard
Chesapeake, VA

Alphabet pasta makes this savory soup fun for kids to eat...and they'll be eating their veggies too!

1 onion, coarsely chopped
2 cloves garlic, minced
2 T. olive oil
1 to 2 T. Italian seasoning
4 c. beef broth
2 c. water

15-oz. can stewed tomatoes
16-oz. pkg. frozen mixed
  vegetables
1/2 c. alphabet pasta, uncooked
salt and pepper to taste
3 T. fresh parsley, minced

In a large soup pot over medium heat, cook onion and garlic in oil until onion is golden, about 8 minutes. Add seasoning to taste; cook and stir for one minute. Add broth, water and tomatoes with juice, breaking tomatoes up as you add them to the pot. Bring to a boil. Reduce heat and simmer for 10 minutes. Stir in mixed vegetables and pasta. Cover and simmer until tender, about 10 to 12 minutes. Add salt and pepper to taste; stir in parsley. Serves 6 to 8.

On a chilly evening, serve soup in prewarmed bowls...a thoughtful touch. Pop oven-safe bowls into a 200-degree oven while the soup simmers. Bowls will be warm in just a few minutes.

SIMMERING Soup Pots

Speedy Chicken Noodle Soup
Vickie

Mom always knows best...a cup of hot chicken soup will have you saying goodbye to the sniffles in no time at all!

1/4 c. onion, diced
1/2 c. celery, thinly sliced
1 t. oil
1/2 c. baby carrots, thinly sliced
4 c. chicken broth

1 c. cooked chicken, chopped
1/2 c. fine egg noodles,
   uncooked
1/2 t. dried parsley
pepper to taste

In a large saucepan over medium heat, sauté onion and celery in oil until tender. Add carrots and broth; bring to a boil. Stir in chicken and noodles. Cook over medium heat for 8 to 10 minutes, until noodles are tender. Stir in parsley and pepper. Makes 3 to 4 servings.

Place a bunch of fresh parsley in the fridge in a water-filled tumbler, covered with a plastic bag. It will keep its just-picked flavor for up to a week, ready to snip into soups and salads.

Oriental Broth with 3 Meats

Lane McLoud
Siloam Springs, AR

Make a savory, warming soup using odds & ends from the fridge.

1 T. butter
2 T. onion, chopped
1 to 2 cloves garlic, minced
2 c. chicken broth
2 c. vegetable broth
1/2 t. salt
1/4 t. pepper

1-1/2 T. soy sauce
1/2 c. cooked ham, chopped
1/2 c. cooked chicken, chopped
1/2 c. cooked shrimp, chopped
1/4 c. canned mushrooms,
   chopped
3 green onions, chopped

Melt butter in a large saucepan over medium heat. Add onion and garlic; sauté for 3 to 5 minutes. Add broths, salt and pepper; bring to a boil. Stir in soy sauce, ham, chicken and shrimp; return to a boil. Add mushrooms and green onions; reduce heat and simmer for 5 minutes. Serves 4.

If there's an extra guest on a soup supper night, just stir in another cup or two of broth, a package of quick-cooking ramen noodles and some frozen peas. Come & get it!

DINNER ON A Bun

Dagwood Burgers

Jennifer Scott
Checotah, OK

When my brother-in-law, Darren, came to visit from Maine, he made these special burgers for our family...we all loved them! Now everyone is requesting this delicious recipe.

2 lbs. lean ground beef
1 lb. Italian ground pork
   sausage
2 c. dry bread crumbs
1 onion, chopped
1/2 c. barbecue sauce

1 egg, beaten
1.35-oz. pkg. onion soup mix
1 t. jalapeño pepper, diced
salt and pepper to taste
12 to 15 hamburger buns, split

Mix all ingredients except salt, pepper and buns in a very large bowl. Form into 12 to 15 patties; sprinkle with salt and pepper. Place on a charcoal grill or in a skillet over medium heat. Cook burgers to desired doneness. Serve on buns. Makes 12 to 15 sandwiches.

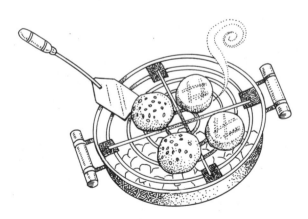

Hamburger buns just taste better toasted...they won't get soggy either. Simply butter buns lightly and place on a hot grill for 30 seconds to one minute or until toasted to taste, turning once.

DINNER ON A Bun

Chet's Bunsteads

Terry Heyndrickx
Morton, IL

My dad loved to cook and would come up with the most scrumptious treats from the ingredients he found around the kitchen. Our favorite sandwich for lunch or dinner was always his Bunstead recipe. I hope you'll love these as much as we kids did!

6-1/2 oz. can tuna, drained
1/4 lb. American cheese, chopped
3 eggs, hard-boiled, peeled and chopped
2 T. green pepper, chopped
2 T. onion, chopped

2 T. green olives with pimentos, chopped
2 T. sweet pickles, chopped
1/2 c. mayonnaise
1 t. seasoning salt
1 t. garlic powder
6 hot dog buns, split

Combine all ingredients except buns; mix well and spoon into buns. Place buns in an aluminum foil-lined 13"x9" baking pan; cover with aluminum foil. Bake at 350 degrees for 30 minutes. Serve warm. Buns may also be cooled, wrapped individually in plastic wrap and refrigerated for the next day's meal. Makes 6 sandwiches.

Frosty strawberry lemonade is refreshing for a summer sandwich supper. Combine a 12-ounce can of frozen lemonade concentrate, a 10-ounce package of frozen strawberries and 4-1/2 cups of cold water in a tall pitcher. Let stand until berries thaw and mix well. Wonderful!

Brown Sugar Barbecues

Kathy Majeske
Denver, PA

*There are many recipes for making barbecues, but this one has been
in my family for as long as I can remember. It's a time-saver...
there's no need to brown the ground beef first.*

1 c. water
3/4 c. catsup
2 T. brown sugar, packed
1 onion, chopped
2 T. mustard

1 T. chili powder
2 t. salt
1 t. pepper
2 lbs. lean ground beef
12 sandwich buns, split

In a large saucepan, mix all ingredients except ground beef and buns.
Bring to a boil over medium heat. Add uncooked beef; simmer for
about 20 to 30 minutes. Spoon onto buns. Serves 12.

Corned Beef Bar-B-Cues

Patt Fleming
Princeton, IL

Perfect for a spur-of-the-moment picnic in the backyard.

2 lbs. ground beef
1 onion, chopped
2 T. all-purpose flour
1 c. water
1 c. catsup

1/4 c. brown sugar, packed
2 t. chili powder
12-oz. can corned beef, chopped
8 hamburger buns, split

In a large skillet over medium heat, brown ground beef and onion;
drain. Stir in flour and water; cook for several minutes, until
thickened. Add catsup, brown sugar, chili powder and corned beef.
Mix well; simmer until hot and bubbly. Serve on buns. Serves 8.

DINNER ON A *Bun*

BLT Quesadilla

Donnie Carter
Wellington, TX

When my niece was recovering from an illness, this recipe was all she wanted to eat. I got more than one phone call from her asking Aunt Donnie to please, please fix another BLT quesadilla.

1 t. butter
2 10-inch flour tortillas
1/3 c. shredded Cheddar Jack
   cheese
2 slices bacon, crisply cooked
   and crumbled

1/2 tomato, chopped
1 to 2 t. onion, chopped
fajita seasoning to taste

Melt butter in a skillet over medium heat; add one tortilla and cook until golden. While tortilla is still in skillet, sprinkle with cheese, bacon, tomato, onion and seasoning. Top with remaining tortilla; turn carefully and cook until golden and cheese has melted. Slice into quarters to serve. Makes one serving.

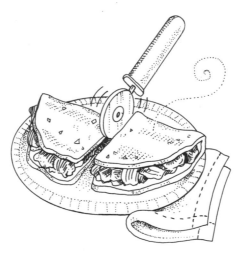

Make your pizza cutter do double duty...it's oh-so handy for slicing cheesy quesadillas into wedges too.

Turkey Gobbler Sandwich

Marion Sundberg
Ramona, CA

I came up with this recipe after my kids decided they liked the pricey "big sandwiches" from the grocery store. Now they like mine best!

1 loaf French bread
1 c. basil pesto sauce
8 slices provolone cheese,
  divided
8 to 10 slices deli turkey breast

2 zucchini, thinly sliced
  lengthwise
1 tomato, thinly sliced
pepper to taste

Slice top 1/4 off loaf and set aside; hollow out bottom of loaf. Spread pesto over insides of both parts of loaf. Layer 4 cheese slices and all of turkey, zucchini and tomato in bottom of loaf; sprinkle with pepper to taste. Arrange remaining cheese slices on top; add top of loaf. Wrap completely in aluminum foil. Grill for 20 to 30 minutes, or until cheese is melted and sandwich is heated through. Unwrap carefully; slice in one-inch slices. Makes 4 to 6 servings.

Grill juicy ripe peaches alongside dinner for an easy, scrumptious dessert. Brush peach halves with melted butter and place cut-side down on a hot grill. Cook for several minutes, until tender and golden. Drizzle with honey or raspberry preserves...luscious!

DINNER ON A Bun

Alberta Prairie Burgers

Shirl Parsons
Cape Carteret, NC

This is a wonderful savory burger from my home of Alberta, Canada. What sets this burger apart from others is the sour cream in the beef mixture, which gives it lots of flavor and juiciness.

1 lb. ground beef
1/2 c. quick-cooking oats, uncooked
1/4 c. light sour cream
1/4 c. mushrooms, minced
1 onion, finely chopped
3 cloves garlic, minced

1 T. Dijon mustard
1 T. fresh parsley, chopped
1 t. dried oregano
1 t. dried thyme
1/4 t. salt
1/4 t. pepper
4 to 6 hamburger buns, split

Combine all ingredients except buns; mix lightly, blending well. Form into 4 to 6 burgers, one to 2 inches thick. Grill on a lightly oiled grill over medium heat for 5 to 7 minutes per side, turning once, to desired doneness. May broil or pan-fry if preferred. Serve on buns. Makes 4 to 6 sandwiches.

Whip up some chive butter to go with ears of roasted sweet corn...a must-have alongside burgers in the summertime! Blend 1/2 cup softened butter with a teaspoon of chopped fresh chives and 1/2 teaspoon minced garlic.

Marty's Special Burgers

Ann Heavey
Bridgewater, MA

Serve these zippy burgers at your next cookout...guests will rave!

1 lb. lean ground beef
2/3 c. crumbled feta or blue
   cheese
1/2 c. bread crumbs
1 egg, beaten

1/2 t. salt
1/4 t. pepper
4 to 6 cherry tomatoes, halved
4 hamburger buns, split

Mix together all ingredients except buns; form into 4 burgers. Grill over high heat to desired doneness, turning to cook on both sides. Serve on buns. Makes 4 sandwiches.

For thick burgers that cook up more quickly and evenly, press your thumb into the center of each patty to form a dime-size hole. The hole will close as the burgers brown.

DINNER ON A Bun

Cobb Salad Subs

JoAnn

A clever twist on an old favorite.

1-1/3 c. cooked chicken, diced
2 roma tomatoes, diced
4 slices bacon, crisply cooked
   and crumbled
1/2 c. crumbled blue cheese
2 eggs, hard-boiled, peeled
   and diced
4 submarine buns, split
   and toasted
4 leaves lettuce

Combine all ingredients except buns and lettuce. Drizzle with Avocado Dressing and toss to coat. Spoon mixture over bottom halves of buns; add lettuce leaves and top halves of buns. Makes 4 sandwiches.

Avocado Dressing:

3 T. olive oil
1 T. white wine vinegar
1 t. Dijon mustard
1/2 t. salt
1/2 t. pepper
1 avocado, pitted, peeled
   and diced

Combine all ingredients except avocado; whisk until well blended. Stir in avocado.

Look for different kinds of breads like multi-grain, sourdough, oatmeal and marble rye...there are so many choices for tasty sandwiches!

Mom's Eggplant Sandwich

Ilene Magee
Staunton, VA

Every time I came home from college, Mom would have these sandwiches ready for me. I still love them to this day.

1 eggplant, sliced 1/2-inch thick
2 zucchini or yellow squash,
    sliced 1/2-inch thick
salt and pepper to taste
2 T. olive oil
3 to 4 T. mayonnaise

1 French baguette loaf, halved
    lengthwise
1 tomato, thinly sliced
1/4 c. grated Parmesan cheese,
    divided

Sprinkle eggplant and squash slices with salt and pepper; set aside. Heat oil in a grill pan over medium heat. Grill eggplant and squash until veggies are tender and have grill marks; drain on a paper towel. Spread mayonnaise over cut sides of loaf. Arrange tomato slices on bottom half; sprinkle with salt, pepper and half of Parmesan cheese. Layer grilled eggplant and squash on top of tomatoes. Sprinkle with remaining cheese and add top half; slice into quarters. Serves 4.

To enjoy the flavor of life, take big bites.
-Robert Heinlein

DINNER ON A Bun

Black Bean Burgers

Amy Pierce
Flower Mound, TX

*These burgers are very good and healthy for you. Served with all the
fixin's, my kids don't even realize there is no meat inside!*

15-oz. can black beans, drained
  and rinsed
1 onion, chopped
1 egg, beaten
1/2 c. dry bread crumbs

1 t. garlic salt
1 t. cayenne pepper
4 whole-wheat buns, split
Garnish: sliced tomatoes,
  Swiss cheese slices

Place black beans and onion in a food processor; process to a
mashed consistency. Transfer to a bowl; mix in egg, bread crumbs
and seasonings. Form into 4 burgers; cook on a grill or in a skillet
for about 5 minutes on each side, until golden. Place on buns; garnish
as desired. Makes 4 sandwiches.

Mild, medium or spicy...salsa is scrumptious on so many more
foods than just tacos. Jazz up plain burgers or hot dogs with a
dollop of salsa instead of catsup...plain no more!

Weekend Treat Burgers

Marie Warner
Jennings, FL

*My husband loves big half-pound burgers, but you could make
6 smaller burgers if your family's appetites are lighter. Top with
sautéed mushrooms for an extra-special meal.*

2/3 c. shredded
  provolone cheese
1/2 c. green pepper, diced
1/2 c. onion, chopped

salt and pepper to taste
2 lbs. ground beef chuck
4 sesame seed kaiser rolls

Toss together cheese, green pepper, onion, salt and pepper in a large
bowl. Add ground beef; mix well and form into 4 burgers. Fry in a
skillet over medium-high heat for 4 to 5 minutes on each side. Serve
on rolls. Serves 4.

Tuck burgers into the pockets of halved pita rounds...
easy for small hands to hold and a tasty change from
the same old hamburger buns.

DINNER ON A Bun

Excellent Burgers

Carrie Kelderman
Pella, IA

This recipe was created on a whim and has become a favorite! Whenever it's prime grilling weather, everyone in the family asks for these burgers. They are so juicy and flavorful that we hardly need all the condiments that we usually pile on.

1 lb. lean ground beef
1 lb. ground pork
2 eggs, beaten

1-1/2 oz. pkg. spaghetti sauce mix
8 hamburger buns, split

Combine all ingredients together except buns. Mix well and form into 8 burgers. Grill over hot coals to desired doneness. Place on buns. Makes 8 sandwiches.

Egg sandwiches make a super-quick and tasty meal. Scramble eggs as you like, tossing in chopped ham or shredded cheese for extra flavor. Serve on toasted, buttered English muffins alongside fresh fruit cups...ready in a flash!

Mom's Pizza Loaf

Linda Thomas
Everett, WA

My mom has made this recipe for as long as I can remember...it was a Saturday night tradition in my family.

1 to 1-1/2 lbs. ground beef
  or turkey
1/2 c. grated Parmesan cheese
1/3 c. green olives with
  pimentos, chopped
1/3 c. onion, chopped
2 6-oz. cans tomato paste

1 t. garlic powder
3/4 t. dried oregano
1 t. salt
1 loaf French bread, halved
  lengthwise
3 tomatoes, thinly sliced
1 lb. sliced Cheddar cheese

Combine uncooked meat, Parmesan cheese, olives, onion, tomato paste and seasonings; mix well. Spread evenly on each half of loaf, making sure to spread to edges. Place both halves on an ungreased baking sheet. Broil about 5 inches from heat for about 12 minutes, or until meat is done. Top with tomato and cheese slices. Return to broiler for one to 2 minutes, just until cheese begins to melt. Slice into serving-size pieces. Serves 8.

Sandwiches are a tasty solution when family members will be dining at different times. Fix sandwiches ahead of time, wrap individually and refrigerate. Pop them into a toaster oven or under a broiler to heat...fresh, full of flavor and ready whenever you are!

DINNER ON A Bun

Billie's Sloppy Joes

Kathleen Sigg
Greeley, CO

This is my ultimate comfort food, one made by my mom back in the 1950's...now it's my grandchildren's favorite too! The poultry seasoning is the "secret ingredient" that makes the Sloppy Joes so delicious.

1 lb. ground beef
1 onion, chopped
10-3/4 oz. can tomato soup
1 t. chili powder
1/2 t. poultry seasoning

1 t. salt
1/2 t. pepper
1 c. shredded Cheddar cheese
6 hamburger buns, split, toasted
 and buttered

In a skillet over medium heat, brown ground beef and onion until onion is translucent. Drain; stir in soup and seasonings. Lower heat; cover and simmer for about 30 minutes, stirring occasionally. Stir in cheese and serve on toasted, buttered hamburger buns. Makes 6 sandwiches.

If the weather is sunny and warm, why not enjoy dinner outdoors? Just toss a red-checked tablecloth on the backyard picnic table and serve sandwiches on paper plates with a big pitcher of sweet tea...relax and enjoy!

Ranch Chicken Wraps

Lea Ann Burwell
Charles Town, WV

*My husband and my children just love these easy-to-make wraps
and request them often.*

4 boneless, skinless chicken
   breasts, sliced into strips
2.8-oz. can French fried onions
1/4 c. bacon bits
8-oz. pkg. shredded Cheddar
   cheese

lettuce leaves
8 to 10 8-inch flour tortillas
Garnish: ranch salad dressing

In a large non-stick skillet over medium heat, cook chicken until
golden and juices run clear. Add onions, bacon bits and cheese to
skillet; cook until cheese melts. Place several lettuce leaves on each
tortilla and spoon chicken mixture on top. Top off with salad dressing
and roll up. Makes 8 to 10 wraps.

Whenever you're grilling chicken for dinner, toss a few extra
boneless, skinless chicken breasts on the grill. Sliced and
refrigerated, they can be served another day in sandwich wraps,
over pasta or topping a hearty salad for an easy meal
with fresh-grilled flavor.

DINNER ON A *Bun*

Greek Chicken Wraps

Tammy Rowe
Bellevue, OH

When my favorite Greek restaurant closed, I just had to try and recreate this recipe, since I had enjoyed it so much.

4 boneless, skinless chicken
   breasts, cut into bite-size
   pieces
1/2 c. Greek vinaigrette salad
   dressing
8-oz. pkg. cream cheese,
   softened
1/4 c. crumbled feta cheese
1 t. dried oregano

1/2 t. dill weed
4 pita rounds or flatbreads,
   warmed
4 lettuce leaves
2 tomatoes, cut into wedges
1 red onion, thinly sliced
7-oz. jar roasted red peppers,
   drained

In a skillet over medium heat, sauté chicken in salad dressing until cooked through and no longer pink. Drain; set aside. Blend cheeses and herbs; spread cheese over warmed bread. Top with lettuce, tomatoes, onion, peppers and chicken. Roll up and slice into 1-1/2 inch pinwheels; serve with Tzatziki Sauce. Makes 4 servings.

Tzatziki Sauce:

8-oz. container sour cream
1 cucumber, peeled and grated
1 onion, grated
1 t. lemon juice

1 t. dried oregano
1 t. dill weed
1 t. salt
1 t. pepper

Mix all ingredients together; serve chilled.

Paper coffee filters make tidy
holders for sandwich wraps
or tacos.

Seaside Salmon Buns

Sharon Velenosi
Garden Grove, CA

Easy, quick and tasty! For a real homestyle treat, substitute
fresh-baked biscuits for the hamburger buns.

14-oz. can salmon, drained and
   flaked
1/4 c. green pepper, chopped
1 T. onion, chopped
2 t. lemon juice

1-1/4 c. mayonnaise, divided
6 hamburger buns, split
12 thick tomato slices
1/2 c. shredded Cheddar cheese

Mix salmon, pepper, onion, lemon juice and 1/2 cup mayonnaise.
Pile salmon mixture onto bun halves; top each with a tomato slice.
Arrange buns on an ungreased baking sheet. Mix remaining
mayonnaise with cheese; spread over tomato slices. Broil until lightly
golden and cheese is melted. Serves 6.

Stir up a dilly of a sauce for salmon patties or crab cakes. Whisk
together 1/2 cup sour cream, one tablespoon Dijon mustard, one
tablespoon lemon juice and 2 teaspoons chopped fresh dill.
Chill...so simple and so good!

DINNER ON A Bun

BLT Tuna Sandwiches

Crystal Wright
Hammond, IN

This is the first recipe I ever made for my beau.
He fell in love with it and requests it at least once a week...
it's so easy that I'm happy to oblige!

7-oz. pkg. white tuna, drained
3 T. bacon bits
1/4 head lettuce, shredded
1 tomato, diced
1/2 to 1 c. mayonnaise

salt and pepper to taste
8 slices multi-grain bread,
  toasted
Garnish: dill pickle spears

Combine tuna, bacon, lettuce and tomato with enough mayonnaise
to achieve desired consistency. Add salt and pepper to taste. Pile tuna
mixture high on 4 bread slices. Top with remaining bread and serve
with pickle spears. Makes 4 sandwiches.

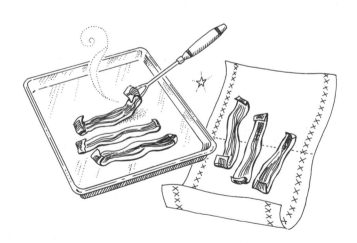

Crispy bacon makes any sandwich a winner! Lay slices on
a jelly-roll pan and bake at 350 degrees for 15 to 20 minutes,
until they're as crisp as you like. Drain well on paper towels.

Island Burgers

Sara Hietpas
Little Chute, WI

Round out this meal like I do, with my homemade French fries and a simple tossed salad. Heavenly!

1 lb. ground beef
1 lb. ground turkey
Optional: 1.35-oz. pkg. onion
  soup mix
seasoned salt to taste
6 to 8 hamburger buns, split
  and toasted

1/2 lb. deli shaved ham,
  warmed
6 to 8 pineapple slices
1/2 c. French salad dressing

Mix beef and turkey together; blend in soup mix, if desired. Form into 6 to 8 burgers. Place on a broiling pan or grill; sprinkle on both sides with seasoned salt. Broil or grill to desired doneness. Serve burgers on toasted buns, topped with ham, a slice of pineapple and a drizzle of salad dressing. Makes 6 to 8 sandwiches.

Baked French Fries:

5 potatoes, peeled and sliced
  into wedges
1 T. canola oil

1.35-oz. pkg. onion soup mix
seasoned salt to taste

Combine all ingredients in a plastic zipping bag. Seal; shake until potatoes are coated. Spread on an ungreased baking sheet. Bake at 400 degrees until potatoes are tender and crispy, 20 to 30 minutes. Makes 5 servings.

Pick up a stack of retro-style plastic burger baskets. Lined with crisp paper napkins, they're still such fun for serving hot dogs, burgers and fries.

Western Burgers

Jennifer Wilken
Bourbonnais, IL

*Both my mom and my grandma served these sandwiches when
I was a child...now I make them for my own family. Top with
a thick slice of onion...yum!*

1 lb. ground beef
1 c. American cheese, cubed
2 T. mustard

1 c. black olives, sliced or
  chopped
4 to 6 hamburger buns, split

Brown ground beef in a skillet over medium heat; drain. Add cheese
to skillet, stirring until melted and mixed well. Add mustard and
olives; mix well. Spoon onto buns to serve. Makes 4 to 6 sandwiches.

Budget-friendly, juicy burgers begin with ground beef chuck.
A little fat in the beef adds flavor...there's no need to purchase
extra-lean sirloin.

Grilled Ham Panini

Tina Goodpasture
Meadowview, VA

Treat yourself to this fast-to-fix sandwich on a busy night. If you don't have a bacon press, weight the sandwich with a small cast-iron skillet.

2 slices sourdough bread
1 T. mayonnaise
6 slices deli smoked ham

2 slices tomato
1 slice American cheese

Spread both slices of bread with mayonnaise on one side. Top one slice with ham, tomato, cheese and remaining bread slice. Spray a griddle or skillet with non-stick vegetable spray. Place sandwich on griddle; set a bacon press or other weight on top. Cook sandwich over medium heat for about 5 minutes, or until lightly golden on both sides. Makes one sandwich.

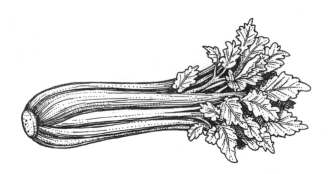

Fill up a relish tray with crunchy fresh cut-up veggies as a simple side dish for sandwiches. A creamy salad dressing can even do double duty as a veggie dip and a sandwich spread.

SPEEDY
Sides

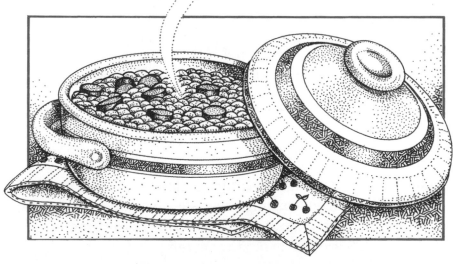

Rosemary & Garlic Potato Hash

Connie Bryant
Topeka, KS

Short on time? Leave the peels on the potatoes like I do...
they add a nice rustic touch.

1/4 c. butter
1-1/4 lbs. russet potatoes,
   peeled and cubed
1 onion, chopped
2 cloves garlic, finely chopped

1/4 c. warm water
1 t. chicken bouillon granules
1 t. dried rosemary
1/4 t. salt
1/8 t. pepper

Melt butter in a large saucepan over medium heat; add remaining ingredients. Mix well and bring to a boil; turn down heat to low. Cover and cook, stirring occasionally, for 20 to 25 minutes, until potatoes are tender. Serves 4.

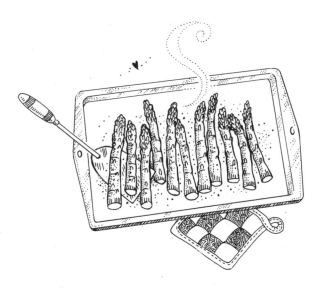

Roasted fresh asparagus is simply delicious...simple to fix too.
Arrange spears on a baking sheet and sprinkle with olive oil
and garlic salt. Bake at 425 degrees for 10 to 15 minutes.
Serve warm or at room temperature.

SPEEDY *Sides*

Susan's Shells & Potatoes

Susan Beckerman
Coral Springs, FL

This simple side dish may not sound like much, but it's delicious and always a special treat! My grandmother used to make this for me when I was a child.

1 potato, peeled and diced
8-oz. pkg. small pasta shells,
    uncooked and divided

2 T. butter, softened
1 t. salt
pepper to taste

Fill a medium saucepan with cold water; add potato. Bring to a boil over high heat. Stir in 2 cups uncooked shells; reserve remaining shells for another recipe. Cook until shells and potato are soft, about 7 to 10 minutes. Drain; toss with butter, salt and pepper. Serves 4.

An easy, cheesy veggie side. Warm 1/3 cup cottage cheese and 2 tablespoons shredded Parmesan cheese in a small saucepan until creamy, then stir in pepper to taste. Spoon over broccoli that's been steamed until crisp-tender.

Garlicky Spinach

Barb Stout
Gooseberry Patch

A super-easy garden-fresh side.

1 T. oil
3 to 4 cloves garlic, thinly sliced

14-oz. pkg. baby spinach
Optional: sliced green onion

In a large skillet over low heat, combine oil and garlic. Cook and stir for several minutes, until garlic is tender. Add spinach; cover and cook for 3 to 4 minutes. Uncover and remove from heat. Toss spinach well; cover again and let stand for an additional 2 minutes. Add salt to taste. Garnish with onion, if desired. Serves 4 to 6.

Italian Green Beans

Amy Lynn Boswell
Xenia, OH

I decided to try something new one evening. Now this is my husband Chad's favorite way to eat green beans! They're delicious with chicken, steak or just about anything.

2 14-1/2 oz. cans green beans
1/2 c. Italian salad dressing

1 t. Italian seasoning

Place beans in a medium saucepan; stir in salad dressing and seasoning. Bring to a boil over medium heat; turn down to a simmer. Cook, stirring occasionally, until most of liquid is gone. Serves 4.

A flavorful drizzle for steamed veggies! Simmer 1/2 cup balsamic vinegar, stirring often, until thickened.
So simple and scrumptious.

Parsley Baked Rice

Patricia Ogilsbie
Canastota, NY

Just a simple fix & forget recipe, but every time I serve it,
someone wants a copy!

3/4 c. long-cooking rice, uncooked
1/2 c. butter, sliced
1-1/2 c. boiling water
2 cubes chicken bouillon

1 to 2 T. dried, minced onion
1 t. dried parsley
1 t. celery seed
1/4 t. salt

Mix all ingredients together; stir until butter is slightly melted. Pour into a 2-quart casserole dish that has been sprayed with non-stick vegetable spray. Cover with aluminum foil. Bake at 350 degrees for 30 minutes. Toss with a fork before serving. Serves 6.

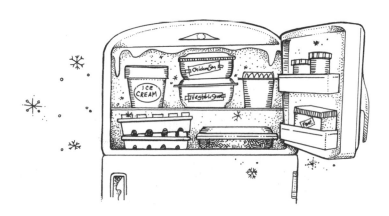

Keep a couple of favorite side dishes tucked away in the freezer for busy days. Pair with hot sandwiches or a deli roast chicken to put a hearty homestyle meal on the table in a hurry.

Fried Apples & Onions

Dawn Hobbs
DeKalb, IL

My grandmother used to eat onions like apples...this dish combines the two favorites together! It goes well with fried pork chops.

2 c. onion, sliced
2 T. butter
2 c. Granny Smith apples, cored,
   peeled and sliced

1/2 c. water
1 t. salt
1/2 t. dried thyme

In a skillet over medium-low heat, cook onions slowly in butter until tender. Add apples, water, salt and thyme. Cover and cook until apples are soft, about 5 to 10 minutes. Uncover; continue cooking until all water is absorbed and apples and onions are lightly golden. Serves 4 to 6.

Don't toss that almost-empty pickle jar...make tangy marinated veggies in a jiffy! Just add cut-up cucumbers, green peppers, carrots, cauliflower and other favorite fresh veggies to the remaining pickle juice and refrigerate. Enjoy within a few days.

SPEEDY *Sides*

Sweet Yammies

Cathy Thomas
British Columbia, Canada

A super-quick way to enjoy this fall favorite.

2 sweet potatoes
1 T. butter, softened

1 T. cinnamon
1-1/2 c. mini marshmallows

Place sweet potatoes on a microwave-safe plate. Microwave on high until very soft, about 10 minutes. Let cool slightly; peel carefully and mash. Combine sweet potatoes, butter and cinnamon; mix well. Spoon into a lightly greased 1-1/2 quart casserole dish; scatter marshmallows over top. Bake, uncovered, at 325 degrees for about 15 minutes, until marshmallows are golden. Serves 4.

Minted peas are a fast and fresh side. Place a small package of frozen baby peas in a skillet over medium heat. Cook and stir until peas are just cooked through. Add one tablespoon butter, 1/2 teaspoon sugar, 2 teaspoons snipped fresh mint and a few drops of lemon juice. Toss until mixed well and serve hot.

Speedy Baked Beans

Mari Bochenek
Lacey, WA

This recipe is amazing! It only takes 10 minutes in the microwave,
yet the beans taste like they've been slow-baked for hours.

16-oz. pkg. bacon, crisply
   cooked and crumbled
2 15-oz. cans pork & beans
1 onion, finely chopped
1/4 c. brown sugar, packed

1/4 c. maple syrup
1/4 c. catsup
1/2 t. dry mustard
1/4 to 1/2 t. cayenne pepper

Stir together all ingredients in a microwave-safe casserole dish.
Cover; microwave on high for 10 minutes. Stir again and serve.
Makes 6 to 10 servings.

To avoid overcooking in the microwave, use round
or oval containers, not square.

SPEEDY *Sides*

Super-Fast Scalloped Potatoes

Lou Ann Peterson
Frewsburg, NY

Believe it or not, I prefer this recipe to the old-fashioned way my grandmother used to make scalloped potatoes. There aren't many modern recipes that I can say that about!

3 T. butter
2 T. all-purpose flour
2 c. milk
salt and pepper to taste

4 c. potatoes, peeled and sliced
1/2 onion, minced
Optional: cubed cooked ham,
   shredded Cheddar cheese

Melt butter in a microwave-safe dish; whisk in flour until smooth. Slowly stir in milk; add salt and pepper. Cover with plastic wrap; microwave on high until mixture begins to thicken, about 8 to 10 minutes, stirring after 4 minutes. Add potatoes and onion; cover tightly. Microwave on high for about 15 minutes. Uncover and stir. Stir in ham and cheese, if desired; cover again. Cook an additional 2 to 3 minutes, until potatoes are tender. Makes 6 to 8 servings.

Sun-warmed ripe tomatoes from the farmers' market...is there anything more irresistible? Serve them simply, drizzled with a little Italian salad dressing and some chopped fresh basil.

Peppers & Pierogies

Cat Bonacchi
Levittown, NY

Serve with grilled sausages for a hearty supper...makes a satisfying meatless main too.

10-oz. pkg. frozen potato and
  onion pierogies
16-oz. pkg. frozen stir-fry
  peppers and onions

8-oz. can tomato sauce
salt and pepper to taste

Cook pierogies according to package directions. Drain, reserving 1/2 cup of cooking liquid; cover pierogies to keep warm. Spray a large sauté pan with non-stick olive oil spray. Add frozen vegetables; cook until tender, golden and most of the liquid is cooked off. Stir in tomato paste and reserved liquid; heat through. Toss sauce mixture with pierogies; add salt and pepper to taste. Serves 3 to 4.

Turn leftover thin spaghetti into tasty noodle patties. Mix
2 to 3 cups cold, cooked pasta with 2 beaten eggs and
1/2 cup ricotta cheese; form into 4 patties. Cook in a skillet in
a little oil until golden, 3 to 4 minutes per side. Serve topped
with warm spaghetti sauce or a sprinkle of Parmesan.

Tomato-Basil Linguine

Judy Dishner
Camden, ME

This simple pasta dish is requested often by my family.
It's easy to toss together...a perfect choice for casual meals.

4 to 5 tomatoes, coarsely
   chopped
1 lb. Cheddar cheese, diced
1/2 to 3/4 c. olive oil
1/2 t. salt

2 to 4 T. dried basil
4 to 5 cloves garlic, minced
16-oz. pkg. linguine pasta,
   cooked

In a large serving bowl, combine all ingredients except pasta, adding basil and garlic to taste. Let stand at room temperature for 30 minutes to 1-1/2 hours. At serving time, add hot cooked pasta and toss well. Serve immediately. Makes 8 to 10 servings.

Jazz up a packaged wild rice mix in a jiffy. Sauté a cup of chopped mushrooms, onion and celery in butter until tender, then add rice mix and prepare as usual.

Mom's Corn Oysters

Susan Tyrie Logsdon
Bowling Green, KY

When I was growing up, my mom would serve these corn "oysters" or fritters for a change from hushpuppies. My friends all wanted to come for supper when Mom made catfish fries and corn oysters!

2 c. creamed or whole corn
2 eggs, beaten
1/2 c. cracker crumbs
1/2 c. all-purpose flour

1/2 t. baking powder
1 t. salt
1/4 t. pepper
oil for frying

Combine corn, eggs and cracker crumbs; set aside. Sift together flour, baking powder, salt and pepper; add to corn mixture and stir well. Heat a small amount of oil in a skillet over medium-high heat. Drop batter into oil by tablespoonfuls, flattening slightly. Pan-fry until golden, about 3 minutes, turning once. Drain on paper towels. Serves 4 to 6.

Buttery herbed potatoes are satisfying and quick to fix. Choose the smallest new potatoes so they'll cook quickly in boiling water. Once potatoes are tender, toss them with butter and snipped fresh chives and parsley.

SPEEDY *Sides*

Weda's Stuffed Tomatoes

Weda Mosellie
Phillipsburg, NJ

Tasty with a broiled steak or fried chicken.

10 roma tomatoes, halved
   lengthwise
1/2 c. shredded mozzarella
   cheese

1/2 c. crumbled feta cheese
1 T. olive oil
pepper to taste
Optional: bread crumbs

Scoop out insides of tomato halves. Mix cheeses together and carefully spoon into tomatoes. Arrange tomatoes in a lightly greased 13"x9" baking pan. Drizzle oil over tomatoes; sprinkle with pepper and bread crumbs, if using. Bake, uncovered, at 375 degrees for 15 to 20 minutes. Makes 10 servings.

Looking for a change from potatoes and rice? Try cornmeal mush...ready-to-use tubes can be found at the supermarket, near the sausage section. Cut into 1/2-inch thick slices and brown in butter or olive oil. Top with warmed spaghetti sauce and sautéed mushrooms. Tasty!

Aunt Marcie's Fried Rice

Kathy Majeske
Denver, PA

My dear aunt gave me this recipe many years ago for my bridal shower.
It's a thrifty, tasty way to use leftover rice.

1/2 lb. bacon, crisply cooked
   and crumbled, 5 T. drippings
   reserved
6 eggs, beaten
1/4 t. salt

3 c. cooked rice, chilled
3/4 c. frozen peas, thawed
1 T. soy sauce
2 T. green onion, sliced

In a large skillet, heat 3 tablespoons reserved drippings until very hot. Beat eggs and salt together with a fork; pour egg mixture into skillet. Cook, stirring quickly and constantly with a spoon until eggs are the size of peas. Reduce heat to low; push eggs to one side of skillet. In same skillet, gently stir rice and remaining drippings until rice is well coated. Add bacon, peas and soy sauce. Gently stir to mix; heat through. Spoon into a serving bowl and sprinkle with green onion. Makes 8 to 10 servings.

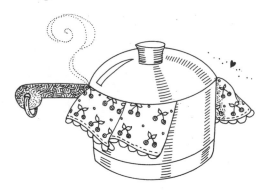

The secret to tender steamed rice! Cook long-cooking rice according to package directions. When it's done, remove pan from heat, cover with a folded tea towel and put lid back on. Let stand for 5 to 10 minutes before serving. The towel will absorb any excess moisture.

SPEEDY *Sides*

Teriyaki Beans & Sprouts

Ellie Brandel
Milwaukie, OR

This is a fun twist for green beans...even kids like them!

1/3 c. onion, chopped
1/4 c. butter
4 c. cooked green beans
16-oz. can bean sprouts,
　drained

4-oz. can chopped mushrooms,
　drained
3 T. soy sauce
Garnish: additional soy sauce

Cook onion in butter until tender. Add beans, sprouts, mushrooms and soy sauce; mix lightly. Simmer, uncovered, for 15 minutes, stirring occasionally. Serve with additional soy sauce, if desired. Serves 4.

Spicy Braised Greens

Jill Burton
Gooseberry Patch

Try Napa or Savoy cabbage in this quick recipe too.

2 T. peanut oil
2 T. garlic, minced
1 T. fresh ginger, peeled
　and grated
1/2 t. red pepper flakes

1 lb. Chinese cabbage or
　bok choy, coarsely chopped
1/4 c. water
soy sauce to taste

Heat oil in a large skillet over medium heat. Add garlic, ginger and red pepper flakes; cook and stir until just beginning to turn golden. Add cabbage; stir to coat. Add water and soy sauce; cover skillet and cook for 3 to 4 minutes, until cabbage is tender. Serves 4 to 6.

Cutting back on salt? Drizzle steamed vegetables with freshly squeezed lemon juice...you'll never miss the salt.

Foolproof Rice Pilaf

Whitney Holbrook
Wilkesboro, NC

You'll love this goof-proof recipe! When I took it to a church carry-in, everyone exclaimed about how delicious it was.

7-oz. pkg. thin spaghetti, uncooked and divided
1/4 c. butter

1 c. long-cooking rice, uncooked
3 c. chicken broth
2 to 3 T. sugar

Break up enough spaghetti to measure 1/2 cup; reserve remaining spaghetti for another recipe. Melt butter in a large saucepan over medium heat. Add broken spaghetti; cook and stir constantly until lightly golden. Add rice; cook and stir until blended. Add broth and sugar to taste. Simmer, covered, over medium heat for 20 to 25 minutes. Makes 5 servings.

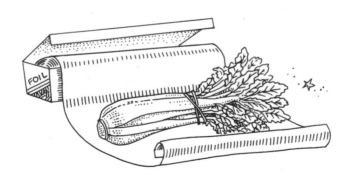

Keep celery crisp and green to the last stalk. Simply remove it from the plastic bag when you bring it home and keep the celery wrapped in aluminum foil.

Toasty Green Beans & Walnuts

Jan Frazier
Louisville, KY

If you wish, replace the shallots with green onions (using the white part only) and a bit of minced garlic.

24-oz. can green beans, drained
1/2 c. chopped walnuts
1 T. olive oil

2 shallots, sliced
1/4 t. salt
1/4 t. pepper

Place beans in a medium saucepan. Add lightly salted water to cover; simmer over medium heat for 5 minutes. Drain and cool. Place nuts in a non-stick skillet over medium-low heat. Cook and stir for about 3 minutes, until toasted. Set aside nuts. Heat oil in same skillet; add shallots and sauté for 5 minutes, until soft. Add beans, nuts, salt and pepper to skillet; toss over medium heat for 2 to 3 minutes. Serves 6.

What was paradise but a garden, full of vegetables
and herbs and pleasures?
-William Lawson

Lemony Linguine

Nicole Shira
New Baltimore, MI

*This is my daughter's favorite recipe! It feeds a crowd but is easy
to cut in half if you're serving just a few people.*

2 16-oz. pkgs. linguine pasta,
   uncooked
1/4 c. butter, sliced
2 egg yolks
2/3 c. whipping cream
1/2 c. grated Parmesan cheese

zest of 1 lemon
juice of 1/2 to 1 lemon
1/8 t. salt
pepper to taste
Optional: 2 to 3 T. fresh parsley,
   chopped

Cook pasta according to package directions; drain and return to pot.
Add butter and stir until pasta is coated; keep warm. Whisk together
remaining ingredients except parsley; stir into pasta. Heat on low for
one to 2 minutes. Sprinkle with parsley, if desired. Serves 8 to 10.

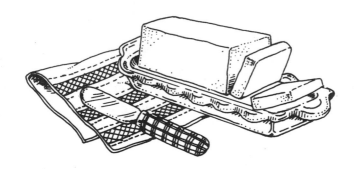

Add a teaspoon or two of butter to the pasta pot...
the pasta won't boil over.

SPEEDY *Sides*

Orzo Garden Medley

Linda Goddard
New Martinsville, WV

*Tiny rice-like orzo pasta cooks up quickly, so it's really handy for
fast-fix sides like this one.*

4 c. water
4 cubes beef bouillon
16-oz. pkg. orzo pasta,
   uncooked and divided
1 T. oil
1 yellow squash, thinly sliced

1 carrot, peeled and shredded
1/2 green pepper, thinly sliced
1/2 onion, thinly sliced
1/2 cucumber, thinly sliced
3 T. Worcestershire sauce

Bring water and bouillon to a boil in a medium saucepan. Measure
1-1/2 cups uncooked orzo, reserving remaining orzo for another recipe.
Add orzo to water and cook to desired tenderness; drain. Heat oil in a
large skillet over medium heat. Add squash, carrot, green pepper and
onion; fry until crisp-tender. Add cucumber and sauce; cook just until
cucumber is warmed. Stir in orzo and heat through. Serves 4 to 6.

Serve seasoned orzo in zucchini boats for a summery side. Cut
zucchini in half lengthwise, scoop out and place in a baking pan.
Bake at 350 degrees for 10 minutes. Fill with orzo mixture and
return to oven until tender and heated through, 8 to 10 minutes.
A clever idea for serving rice or stuffing too!

Crispy Baked Eggplant

Phyllis Peters
Three Rivers, MI

Serve with warm marinara sauce.

2 T. oil
1 eggplant, sliced 1/2-inch thick

2 eggs, beaten
1 c. biscuit baking mix

Brush oil over a baking sheet; set aside. Dip eggplant slices into eggs and coat with baking mix; arrange on baking sheet. Bake at 375 degrees on top rack of oven for 15 minutes; turn over and bake an additional 15 minutes, until golden and tender. Serves 4.

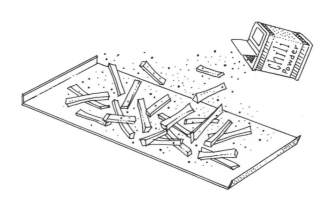

Sweet potato fries are deliciously different! Slice sweet potatoes into strips or wedges, toss with olive oil and place on a baking sheet. Bake at 400 degrees for 20 to 30 minutes until tender, turning once. Sprinkle with a little cinnamon-sugar.

Parmesan Zucchini Sticks

Marion Sundberg
Ramona, CA

Serve instead of French fries alongside cheeseburgers...kids will gobble them up!

1 egg
1/2 c. Italian-flavored dry
   bread crumbs
1/2 c. grated Parmesan cheese

1 t. dried thyme
1/2 t. pepper
4 zucchini, quartered lengthwise
Garnish: ranch salad dressing

Whisk egg in a shallow bowl; set aside. Mix bread crumbs, cheese, thyme and pepper in a separate bowl. Dip zucchini into egg and then into crumb mixture. Place on a baking sheet sprayed with non-stick vegetable spray. Bake at 450 degrees for 20 to 25 minutes, until tender. Serve with ranch salad dressing or your favorite dipping sauce. Serves 4.

Whip up a yummy Parmesan dip to serve with French fries and veggie sticks. Combine 1/2 cup mayonnaise, 1/4 cup grated Parmesan cheese, 1/2 teaspoon dried basil and 1/4 teaspoon garlic powder. The dip's flavor is even better if made ahead of time and chilled.

Sweet & Nutty Couscous

Amy Bell
Arlington, TN

A deliciously different side dish for dinner...we even enjoy it for breakfast instead of oatmeal.

2 c. vegetable broth
5 T. butter, sliced
1/2 c. dates, chopped
1/2 c. dried apricots, chopped

1/2 c. golden raisins
2 c. couscous, uncooked
1/2 c. slivered almonds, toasted
1 T. cinnamon

Pour broth into a large saucepan; bring to a boil over medium-high heat. Add butter, dates, apricots and raisins; boil for 2 to 3 minutes. Remove from heat; stir in couscous. Cover and let stand 5 minutes. Stir in almonds and cinnamon. Makes 4 to 6 servings.

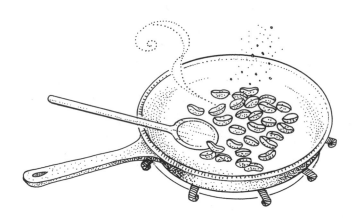

Toasting really brings out the flavor of shelled nuts...and it's oh-so-easy! Place nuts in a small dry skillet. Cook and stir over low heat for a few minutes until toasty and golden... it's that simple!

German Potato Pancakes

Elaine Nichols
Mesa, AZ

Garnish with sour cream or applesauce...scrumptious!

4 potatoes, peeled and coarsely
   grated
1/4 c. milk
1 egg, beaten

1 onion, diced
2 T. all-purpose flour
salt and pepper to taste
oil for frying

Combine all ingredients except oil; mix well with a fork and set aside.
Heat 1/4 inch oil in a deep skillet over medium-high heat. For each
pancake, spread about 2 heaping tablespoonfuls into a circle in skillet.
Cook for 3 to 4 minutes, until golden; turn and cook on other side.
Drain on paper towels. Serves 4 to 6.

Homemade applesauce is a natural partner for pork chops.
Core, peel and chop four tart apples and place in a saucepan
with 1/4 cup brown sugar, 1/4 cup water and 1/2 teaspoon
cinnamon. Cook over medium-low heat for 8 to 10 minutes,
until soft. Mash with a potato masher and serve warm,
dusted with a little more cinnamon.

Kristen's Baked Beans

Kristen Lewis
Bourbonnais, IL

Worthy of Grandma's hand-me-down bean pot.

15-oz. can pork & beans
1 t. mustard
1 T. dried, minced onion

1/4 c. catsup
1/4 c. brown sugar, packed

Combine all ingredients; mix well and pour into a greased
8"x8" casserole dish. Bake, uncovered, at 350 degrees for 30 minutes.
Serves 4 to 6.

Country Beans & Potatoes

Lorrie Smith
Drummonds, TN

This is one of my husband's favorites. Add a cup or two
of ham cubes for a heartier dish.

2 15-oz. cans green beans
2 15-oz. cans sliced potatoes,
    drained

1 onion, chopped
1 T. bacon drippings
salt and pepper to taste

Combine beans in their liquid, potatoes and remaining ingredients in
a large saucepan; stir well. Bring to a boil over medium-high heat.
Reduce heat; cover and simmer for about 20 minutes, until onion is
translucent. Serves 4 to 6.

For extra-fluffy white rice, just add
a teaspoon of white vinegar to
the cooking water.

SPEEDY *Sides*

Colorful Rice Toss

Keersten Jensen
Idaho Falls, ID

One day while I was in college, I tried this recipe because I didn't have the ingredients to make fried rice. When I took a taste, I couldn't get enough of it! I have been making this rice for over 20 years now. It's especially good with chicken...we like it hot or cold!

2 c. instant rice, uncooked
2 c. boiling water
1 to 2 T. butter
1 onion, chopped

8-oz. bottle zesty Italian salad
   dressing
1 tomato, chopped

Stir rice into boiling water; cover and let stand for 5 minutes, or until water is absorbed. Melt butter in a frying pan over medium heat; cook onion until translucent. Add rice to pan; pour salad dressing over, stirring to coat. Remove from heat and stir in tomato. Serve warm or chilled. Serves 4 to 6.

Serve up a veggie plate for dinner...a good old Southern tradition. With 2 or 3 scrumptious veggie dishes and a basket of buttery cornbread, no one will miss the meat!

Saucy Zucchini & Tomatoes

Gerry Donnella
Boston, VA

Remember this recipe when you have a bumper crop of zucchini in your garden! Serve with crusty bread and a tall glass of icy sweet tea for a delightfully simple lunch.

2 T. bacon drippings
1 onion, sliced
1 c. tomatoes, chopped

1/2 bay leaf
salt and pepper to taste
3 zucchini, sliced 1-inch thick

Heat drippings in a skillet over medium heat. Add onion; sauté until transparent. Add tomatoes, bay leaf, salt and pepper; simmer for 5 minutes. Add zucchini; cover and simmer until tender, about 8 to 10 minutes. Discard bay leaf before serving. Serves 4 to 6.

Cook egg noodles the easy way, no watching needed.
Bring water to a rolling boil, then turn off heat. Add noodles
and let stand for 20 minutes, stirring twice.

SPEEDY *Sides*

Pan-Fried Oven Potatoes

Patricia Tilley
Sabine, WV

A very old dish my grandmother used to make. She was always canning, baking or making candy and was dearly loved by family & friends.

6 to 8 potatoes, peeled and
   halved

3 T. butter, melted
4 to 6 slices bacon

Cook potatoes in boiling salted water until fork-tender; drain. Coat a cast-iron skillet with melted butter. Place potatoes in skillet; arrange uncooked bacon slices on top. Bake, covered, at 425 degrees for 25 minutes. Serves 6 to 8 people.

Quick Oniony Potatoes

Judy Paintner
Happy Valley, OR

My sister-in-law gave me this yummy recipe for potatoes. My husband and son love to dip them in Thousand Island salad dressing.

6 redskin potatoes, cubed
1 T. olive or canola oil

1.35-oz. pkg. onion soup mix

Place potatoes in a microwave-safe casserole dish. Sprinkle with oil and soup mix; toss to mix. Microwave, covered, on high for 5 minutes. Stir; return to microwave for an additional 10 to 15 minutes, or until tender. Serves 4.

For extra-creamy mashed potatoes, stir in some fat-free cream cheese.

Creamy Italian Noodles

Beth Shaeffer
Greenwood, IN

These zesty noodles are so quick & easy to prepare...a super alternative to rice or potatoes.

8-oz. pkg. thin egg noodles,
    uncooked
1/4 c. butter, sliced
1/2 c. evaporated milk or
    half-and-half

1/4 c. grated Parmesan cheese
2-1/4 t. Italian salad
    dressing mix

Prepare egg noodles according to package directions; drain and set aside. In the same saucepan, melt butter. Return noodles to pan and add milk or half-and-half and cheese. Stir to combine; add dressing mix and stir again. Serves 4.

Steam crisp-tender vegetables in the microwave. Place cut-up veggies in a microwave-safe container and add a little water. Cover with plastic wrap, venting with a knife tip. Microwave on high for 2 to 5 minutes, checking for tenderness after each minute. Uncover carefully to allow hot steam to escape.

CRUSTY BREAD & A *Salad*

Pamm's Deluxe Garlic Bread

Pamela Delacruz
Mount Vernon, WA

*For a time, we attended church services in the home of a friend, followed
by a meal together. This bread was often requested...it was always
snatched up as soon as it was cool enough to eat!*

8-oz. pkg. cream cheese,
  softened
1/4 c. butter, softened
4 to 5 green onions, chopped
4-oz. can chopped black olives,
  drained

2 t. garlic, minced
1 T. Italian seasoning
1 loaf French bread, halved
  lengthwise

Combine all ingredients except bread; blend well. Spread mixture
evenly on both halves of bread. Place on an ungreased baking sheet.
Bake at 350 degrees for 10 to 15 minutes, until bubbly and golden.
Allow to cool; cut each half into 6 slices. Makes 12 servings.

If a recipe calls for softened butter, grate chilled sticks with
a cheese grater. The butter will soften in just minutes.

CRUSTY BREAD & A *Salad*

Moose's Garden Salad

Patti Barnett
Hillsboro, MO

*My husband wanted to try something different after harvesting
bushels of fresh tomatoes and cukes from the garden...
this zesty tasting salad was the result.*

2 tomatoes, diced
1 cucumber, peeled and diced
1/2 onion, diced
salt and pepper to taste

1/2 c. crumbled feta cheese
2-1/4 oz. can sliced black olives,
    drained
2 T. Greek salad dressing

Combine tomatoes, cucumber and onion in a serving bowl; sprinkle
with salt and pepper to taste. Add cheese, olives and salad dressing;
toss well. Serve immediately, or refrigerate up to 2 days. Serves 6.

Mix up a crunchy salad fast with no dishes to wash. Toss lettuce,
veggies and any other toppers in a one-gallon plastic zipping
bag...give it a shake and pour into salad bowls.

Strawberry Vinaigrette

JoAnn

Drizzle on grilled chicken...heavenly!

1 c. strawberry preserves
1/4 c. balsamic vinegar
1/4 c. Dijon mustard
1/2 t. pepper

1/2 c. olive oil
1/2 c. white wine or white
   grape juice

Whisk together preserves, vinegar, mustard and pepper until well blended. Gradually whisk in oil and wine or juice. Cover; keep refrigerated. Makes about 2-1/2 cups.

Raspberry Vinaigrette

Melody Taynor
Everett, WA

Toss with bite-size fresh fruit for a refreshing summer salad.

1/4 c. olive oil
1 c. cider vinegar or seasoned
   rice vinegar

10-oz. jar seedless red raspberry
   jam

Combine all ingredients in a blender; process until smooth. Cover; keep refrigerated. Makes about 2-1/2 cups.

Creamy fat-free vanilla yogurt makes a luscious topping for fresh strawberries, nectarines and blueberries. For an extra taste treat, drizzle with fruit-flavored vinaigrette.

CRUSTY BREAD & A *Salad*

Hula Salad

Gretchen Brown
Forest Grove, OR

A refreshing salad that's easily stirred up any time of year.

7 c. lettuce, torn
8-oz. can pineapple chunks,
    drained and 1 T. juice
    reserved

1 c. shredded Cheddar cheese
1/2 c. mayonnaise
1 T. sugar

In a large salad bowl, toss together lettuce, pineapple and cheese; set aside. In a small bowl, combine mayonnaise, sugar and reserved pineapple juice; mix well. Pour over salad; toss to coat. Serve immediately. Serves 6.

Moderation. Small helpings. Sample a little bit of everything.
These are the secrets of happiness and good health.
-Julia Child

Simply Coleslaw

Jill Ball
Highland, UT

My children love coleslaw...really! So we eat it often. I put it on grilled chicken, poorboy sandwiches and fish tacos. This recipe is good enough to enjoy all by itself, though...the pineapple and carrots give it a pleasing sweetness.

1 head cabbage, chopped
4 carrots, peeled and grated
1 onion, chopped
8-oz. can sliced pineapple,
   drained and chopped

1 c. plain low-fat yogurt
salt and pepper to taste
Optional: garlic powder and
   paprika to taste

In a large serving bowl, mix cabbage, carrots, onion, pineapple and yogurt. Add salt and pepper to taste; if desired, add garlic powder and paprika. Chill for 30 minutes before serving. Serves 6.

Don't toss out that dab of leftover cranberry sauce! Purée it with balsamic vinaigrette to create a tangy salad dressing.

CRUSTY BREAD & A *Salad*

Diane's Skillet Cornbread

Diane Girard
Asheboro, NC

An elderly neighbor friend had been making this recipe for years, and got me to taste it...one taste and I was hooked! If you like a sweet, moist cornbread, you'll love this one.

1/2 c. margarine
2 8-1/2 oz. pkgs. corn muffin
   mix, divided
1/3 c. sugar

3 eggs, beaten
1/2 c. milk
Garnish: additional melted
   margarine

Place margarine in a cast-iron skillet; melt in a 350-degree oven. Place 1-1/2 packages muffin mix in a large bowl, reserving remaining mix for another recipe. Stir in sugar, eggs and milk; mix well and pour in melted margarine from skillet. Stir; pour batter into skillet. Bake at 350 degrees for 30 minutes, or until light golden. Brush top with margarine; cut into wedges and serve hot. Serves 8.

Honey butter is delectable melting into warm cornbread.
Simply blend 2/3 cup honey with 1/2 cup softened butter.

Lemony Caesar Dressing

Sandy Minten
Klamath Falls, OR

It takes just a minute to whisk together this super-fresh dressing.

1/2 c. olive oil
3 T. lemon juice
2 cloves garlic, minced

1 t. Dijon mustard
1/2 t. salt
1/8 t. pepper

Blend all ingredients until smooth. Keep refrigerated. Makes about
3/4 cup.

Tuscan Dipping Oil

Denise Webb
Galveston, IN

Set out small dishes of this flavorful oil and some crusty Italian bread...
no one will mind waiting until dinner has finished cooking!

1 t. red pepper flakes
1 t. dried oregano
1 t. dried rosemary
1 t. dried basil
1 t. dried parsley

1 t. garlic, minced
1 t. granulated garlic
1 t. kosher salt
1 t. pepper
1/2 c. olive oil

Combine all ingredients except oil; mix well. At serving time, stir in
oil. Makes about 3/4 cup.

What kind of olive oil to use?
Reserve extra-virgin olive oil
for delicately flavored salad
dressings and dipping sauces.
Less-expensive light olive oil
is fine for cooking.

CRUSTY BREAD & A *Salad*

Tomato-Basil Salad

Jami Rodolph
Stevensville, MT

*Really yummy! I love to make this salad after I've been to the farmers'
market to buy sun-warmed fresh tomatoes, basil and garlic.*

8 ripe tomatoes, chopped
1 T. garlic, chopped
10 leaves fresh basil, torn
2 T. olive oil

2 T. balsamic vinegar
1 t. kosher salt, or more to taste
1 t. coarse pepper

Mix tomatoes, garlic and basil in a salad bowl. Drizzle with oil and
vinegar; stir. Add salt and pepper and stir again. Let stand 30 minutes
before serving. Makes 6 to 8 servings.

Serve up a do-it-yourself salad bar when summer fun beckons.
Alongside a large bowl of crisp greens, set out muffin tins filled
with chopped veggies, diced hard-boiled egg, grilled sliced
chicken, shredded cheese and creamy dressings. A basket of hot
rolls and a pitcher of icy lemonade rounds out the menu...dig in!

Sharon's Banana Muffins

Sharon Wood
West Columbia, SC

I have used this recipe since my daughter was a baby...she enjoyed making these herself when I was teaching her to cook. She is now 29 years old and her children are learning to bake under my supervision too. Enjoy making your own memories!

1/2 c. butter, softened
1 c. sugar
2 eggs, beaten
3/4 c. ripe banana, mashed

1-1/4 c. all-purpose flour
3/4 t. baking soda
1/2 t. salt

Blend butter and sugar; add eggs and beat well. Stir in banana; set aside. Sift together flour, baking soda and salt; add to butter mixture and mix until moistened. Fill paper-lined muffin cups 2/3 full. Bake at 350 degrees for 25 to 30 minutes. If preferred, use a greased and floured 9"x5" baking pan; bake for an additional 5 to 10 minutes. Makes 8 to 10 muffins or one loaf.

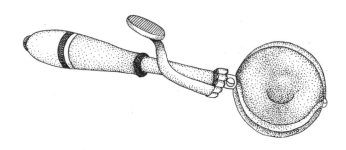

A retro-style ice cream scoop with a lever is just right for filling muffin cups with batter.

CRUSTY BREAD & A *Salad*

Cinnamon-Apple Muffins

Linda Davidson
Lexington, KY

These muffins are scrumptious served warm with butter...they make any meal a little more special!

2 c. all-purpose flour
1 T. baking powder
1/8 t. salt
1 t. cinnamon
1/2 t. allspice
3 T. brown sugar, packed
3 T. butter, melted

3/4 c. milk
2 T. mayonnaise
2 apples, cored, peeled
   and grated
1/3 c. raisins
1/3 c. chopped walnuts

Sift flour, baking powder, salt and spices into a medium bowl. Add remaining ingredients and mix well; batter will be thick. Spoon batter into 12 paper-lined muffin cups. Bake at 400 degrees until firm to the touch, about 20 minutes. Transfer to a wire rack to cool slightly; serve warm. Makes one dozen.

Mix up a zesty Dijon dressing in an almost-empty mustard jar... it's easy! Pour 3 tablespoons olive oil, 2 tablespoons cider vinegar and a clove of minced garlic into the jar, replace the lid and shake well. Add salt and pepper to taste. Delicious drizzled over mixed greens or broiled fish.

Sweet Potato Cornbread

Valarie Dennard
Palatka, FL

*Savor this cornbread like my family does...smothered in
butter and honey!*

2 c. self-rising cornmeal mix
1/4 c. sugar
1 t. cinnamon
1 c. sweet potato, peeled,
   cooked and mashed

1-1/2 c. milk
1/4 c. butter, melted and slightly
   cooled
1 egg, beaten

Stir together all ingredients, whisking just enough to moisten.
Spoon into a greased 8" cast-iron skillet or round baking pan.
Bake at 425 degrees for 20 to 25 minutes. Cut into wedges to serve.
Makes 6 servings.

Keep bags of sweetened dried cranberries and chopped walnuts
tucked in the cupboard for healthy between-meal snacking.
A quick toss of nuts & berries really dresses up a
plain-Jane salad in a snap too.

CRUSTY BREAD & A *Salad*

Broccoli-Cashew Slaw

Kerry Schulz
Myerstown, PA

Mmm...creamy slaw with a triple crunch of broccoli,
crispy bacon and cashews!

1/2 c. mayonnaise
1/4 c. half-and-half
1/4 c. grated Parmesan cheese
1 T. sugar
salt and pepper to taste

16-oz. pkg. broccoli slaw mix
3 to 4 slices bacon, crisply
 cooked and crumbled
1/2 c. cashew halves

In a large bowl, combine mayonnaise, half-and-half, cheese, sugar, salt and pepper; mix until well blended. Add slaw and toss to mix; stir in bacon and cashews. Serve immediately or chill. Serves 6.

Add some finely chopped bread & butter pickles to your next coleslaw for a zippy new taste.

Amy's Sweet & Super Dressing

Amy Wrightsel
Louisville, KY

My most-requested recipe at office cookouts. Drizzle over fresh baby spinach or mixed salad greens tossed with chopped pecans, crisp bacon, mushrooms and cherry tomatoes...delightful!

1 c. olive oil
1/3 c. cider vinegar
1/4 c. sweet onion, minced
1/2 c. sugar

1 t. dry mustard
1 t. celery seed
1 t. salt

Mix all ingredients together in a tightly lidded container. Shake until well blended; keep refrigerated. Makes about 2 cups.

Keep baking soda on hand for removing soil, wax and residue from fresh fruit and vegetables. Sprinkle a little baking soda on dampened produce, scrub gently and rinse with cool water... no fancy produce washes needed.

Apple Orchard Salad

Debra Manley
Bowling Green, OH

*Chock-full of sweet fruit, this ambrosial salad will make
the most ordinary meal special.*

1-1/2 c. Golden Delicious
   apples, cored, peeled and
   diced
1-1/2 c. Red Delicious apples,
   cored, peeled and diced
2 T. lemon juice
1 c. celery, chopped
1 c. red seedless grapes, halved

1 c. mini marshmallows
1/2 c. chopped pecans
1/4 c. raisins
2/3 c. mayonnaise
2/3 c. frozen whipped topping,
   thawed
1/4 c. sugar
1/4 t. nutmeg

In a large bowl, toss apples with lemon juice. Add celery, grapes,
marshmallows, pecans and raisins. In a separate small bowl, mix
remaining ingredients; fold into apple mixture. Serve immediately or
chill. Makes 6 to 8 servings.

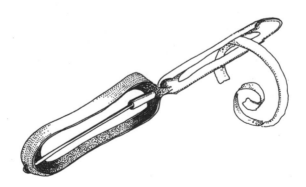

Make cheese curls quickly for garnishing salads...simply pull
a vegetable peeler across the block of cheese.

French Onion Biscuits

Lane Ann Miller
Hopkinsville, KY

These biscuits are quick, easy and scrumptious...wonderful with soups or Italian dishes.

8-oz. container French onion dip   2 c. biscuit baking mix
1/4 c. milk   1 T. butter, melted
1 t. dried parsley

In a large bowl, whisk together onion dip, milk and parsley until smooth. Stir in baking mix until well blended. Drop dough by spoonfuls onto a lightly greased baking sheet, making 12 biscuits. Bake at 450 degrees for 7 to 8 minutes, or until lightly golden. Immediately brush tops of biscuits with melted butter. Makes one dozen.

A pat of herb butter makes delicious food taste even better. Simply blend chopped fresh herbs into softened butter and spoon into a crock. Choose from parsley, dill, tarragon and chives, or create your own herb garden mixture.

CRUSTY BREAD & A *Salad*

Homemade Ranch Dressing

Sandy Roy
Crestwood, KY

More than a salad dressing...a yummy dip for carrots, celery stalks and other fresh veggies.

1 c. mayonnaise
1/2 c. sour cream
1/2 t. dried chives
1/2 t. dried parsley
1/2 t. dill weed

1/4 t. garlic powder
1/4 t. onion powder
1/8 t. salt
1/8 t. pepper

Whisk all ingredients together in a medium bowl. Cover and chill for at least 30 minutes, so flavors can blend. Keep refrigerated. Makes about 1-1/2 cups.

Speedy salad topper! An egg slicer makes short work of slicing mushrooms and olives as well as hard-boiled eggs. It can turn out uniform slices of soft fruit like strawberries and bananas too.

Red, Green & White Salad

Barbara Imler
Portland, IN

Not your usual tossed salad! Crunchy veggies and greens
are topped with a rich, creamy dressing.

1 head cauliflower, cut into
   flowerets and thinly sliced
1 c. radishes, sliced

1/2 c. watercress or baby
   spinach, finely sliced
2 T. green onion, thinly sliced

Toss all ingredients together in a large salad bowl. Drizzle with
Parmesan Dressing to taste; toss well. Serves 4 to 6.

Parmesan Dressing:

1/2 c. sour cream
1/2 c. mayonnaise
2 T. olive oil
2 T. grated Parmesan cheese
juice of 1/2 lemon

1 clove garlic, minced
1/8 t. cayenne pepper
1/2 t. salt
1/8 t. pepper

Combine ingredients well. Cover; keep refrigerated.

An oldie but goodie that's ready to serve in seconds...spoon
blue cheese or Thousand Island salad dressing over crisp
wedges of iceberg lettuce. Sprinkle with chopped tomato
and crispy bacon...yum!

CRUSTY BREAD & A *Salad*

Blue Cheese Dressing

Carolyn Ritz Wade
Hayesville, NC

If you love rich-tasting blue cheese like I do, you'll want to
make this your very own house dressing!

4-oz. container crumbled blue
   cheese
3 T. mayonnaise
1/4 c. sour cream

1 T. white vinegar
3/4 t. Dijon mustard
3 to 4 T. olive oil
salt and pepper to taste

Mash cheese with a fork. Add mayonnaise, sour cream, vinegar and
mustard; mix until well blended but not smooth. Whisk in oil; add
salt and pepper to taste. Keep refrigerated in a covered container.
Makes one cup.

Thousand Island Dressing

Nancy Girard
Chesapeake, VA

Try this dressing with seafood or dolloped on your next
Reuben sandwich...out of this world!

1 c. mayonnaise
1/4 c. catsup
1 T. seasoned rice vinegar

2 t. sugar
2 T. sweet pickle relish

Combine all ingredients together; mix well. Cover and refrigerate until
ready to use. Makes 1-1/2 cups.

Tomatoes will ripen quickly when placed together with
a banana in a brown paper grocery bag.

Corn & Green Chile Muffins

Sandy Nobles
Petal, MS

Let a bandanna-lined basket of these spicy muffins star at your next
chili supper...stand back and wait for the compliments!

1-1/4 c. cornmeal
1/2 t. salt
2 t. baking powder
1 c. shredded sharp Cheddar
   cheese
8-oz. can creamed corn

4-oz. can chopped green chiles,
   drained
8-oz. container sour cream
2 eggs, beaten
1/4 c. canola oil

Combine cornmeal, salt and baking powder; mix well. Stir in cheese,
corn, chiles and sour cream. Add eggs and oil; stir just until combined.
Spoon batter into a muffin tin that has been sprayed with non-stick
vegetable spray, filling each cup about 1/2 full. Bake at 400 degrees
for about 20 minutes, until golden. Makes one dozen.

A warm fruit compote is a delightful change from tossed salads.
Simmer cut-up peaches, blueberries and raspberries together
with a little honey, lemon juice and cinnamon, just until
syrupy and tender. Divine made with fresh summer fruit...
in wintertime, frozen fruit is scrumptious too.

CRUSTY BREAD & A *Salad*

Ruby's 3-Bean Salad

Hope Davenport
Portland, TX

*When going through some of my grandma's things, I ran across some
very old recipes of hers...the paper is brown with age and very tattered.
This oh-so-simple yet tasty recipe was among them.*

14-1/2 oz. can green beans,
   drained
14-1/2 oz. can yellow wax
   beans, drained
16-oz. can kidney beans,
   drained and rinsed

2/3 c. vinegar
1/3 c. oil
1 c. sugar

Combine all ingredients in a serving bowl. Let stand for 30 minutes,
or refrigerate overnight for best flavor. Drain well before serving.
Serves 8 to 10.

Salad smarts! The darker the greens, the healthier they are
for you. Try spinach or romaine lettuce...if iceberg lettuce is
more to your liking, try a mix of iceberg and darker greens.

Cheesy Garlic Bread

Gen Mazzitelli
Binghamton, NY

I love to serve this yummy bread with my homemade beef stew...it's a "must" alongside any favorite pasta dish too.

1/4 c. canola oil
2 T. fresh parsley, minced
1 T. garlic, minced
1/2 t. salt

1/4 t. pepper
1 loaf French or Italian bread,
    halved lengthwise
grated Parmesan cheese to taste

Combine oil, parsley, garlic, salt and pepper in a small bowl. Spread mixture over bread halves; place on a baking sheet that has been lightly sprayed with non-stick vegetable spray. Bake at 400 degrees for 5 to 8 minutes, until bread is hot and lightly golden. Immediately sprinkle generously with cheese. Slice each half into 6 slices. Makes 12 servings.

Freshen up day-old bread in a jiffy. Just sprinkle the loaf with water and bake at 400 degrees for 6 to 8 minutes.

CRUSTY BREAD & A *Salad*

Tomato Delight Dressing

Patsy Ball
Marlow, OK

A zesty buttermilk dressing that's lovely with
ripe red tomatoes and crisp lettuce.

32-oz. jar mayonnaise
1 c. buttermilk
1/4 c. catsup
1/4 c. vinegar

1/4 c. sugar
1 T. garlic powder
3/4 t. salt

Mix together all ingredients in a large bowl. Cover; keep refrigerated.
Makes about 6 cups.

Mix up your own Italian seasoning for pasta dishes, soups, salad
and garlic bread. A good basic blend is two tablespoons each of
dried oregano, thyme, basil, marjoram and rosemary...add or
subtract to suit your family's taste. Store in a big shaker jar.

Mother's Pull-Apart Cheese Bread

Lori Vincent
Alpine, UT

*My mother always made this cheese bread for family get-togethers.
Although she is no longer with us, I reach for this buttery, savory
bread whenever I need to feel closer to her.*

1 loaf unsliced white bakery
   bread
8-oz. pkg. shredded pasteurized
   process cheese spread
1/2 c. butter, softened and
   divided

1-1/2 t. onion, finely chopped
1 t. Worcestershire sauce
1/4 t. celery seed

Trim crust off top and sides of loaf with a long serrated knife. Cut loaf
into 1-1/2 inch slices without cutting through bottom crust. Cut across
slices from end to end, forming 1-1/2 inch squares. Combine cheese,
1/4 cup butter, onion, sauce and celery seed; spread between squares.
Melt remaining butter; brush over top and sides of loaf. Place on an
ungreased baking sheet. Bake at 350 degrees for 20 to 25 minutes,
until hot and golden. Makes 10 to 12 servings.

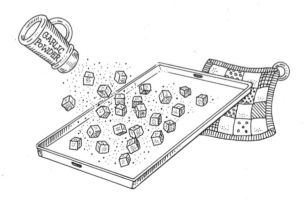

It's thrifty to turn leftover bread into toasty salad croutons.
Toss bread cubes with olive oil, garlic powder and dried herbs.
Bake on a baking sheet at 400 degrees for 5 to 10 minutes,
until golden and toasty.

CRUSTY BREAD & A *Salad*

Mom's Tomato Thing

Sandy Carpenter
Washington, WV

This is a great side dish for meats, even burgers, but the very best way to enjoy it is to dip French bread into the juices. It's almost a meal in itself!

1 clove garlic, halved lengthwise
4 ripe tomatoes, diced
1 white or red onion, finely
   chopped

2 t. sugar
1 t. dried basil
1/4 c. vinegar
3 T. oil

Rub cut side of garlic halves over the inside of a salad bowl; discard garlic. Add tomatoes and onion to bowl; set aside. Mix together sugar, basil, vinegar and oil until sugar is dissolved. Add to tomato mixture; let stand for about 30 minutes to one hour. Makes 4 servings.

Warm soft pretzels can go from oven to table in minutes...it's child's play! Twist strips of refrigerated bread stick dough into pretzel shapes and place on an ungreased baking sheet. Brush with beaten egg white, sprinkle with coarse salt and bake as directed.

Eric's Favorite Sauce

Denise Neal
Castle Rock, CO

This dressing is how I got Eric, my "I hate salad" kid, to eat salad.
It does double duty as a veggie dip for an appetizer...try it with baby
carrots and sugar snap peas! We really prefer it over the traditional
ranch dressing or sour cream dip.

1/2 c. canola oil	1/4 c. honey
1/4 c. red wine vinegar	1 t. Dijon mustard
1/4 c. creamy peanut butter	1/4 t. salt

Combine all ingredients in a jar; cover and shake until well blended.
Store in refrigerator. Makes about 1-1/4 cups.

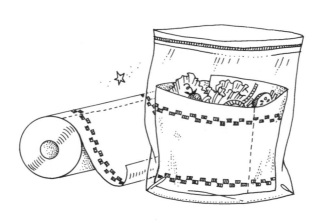

Toss together salads for several days' meals so dinner is
quick & easy. Store salad greens in a plastic zipping bag,
tuck in a paper towel to absorb extra moisture and refrigerate.
They'll stay crisp for up to 4 days.

Desserts IN A JIFFY

Berry Peachy Twists

Cyndy Wilber
Ravena, NY

*I've been making this treat for our family for almost 40 years. It is
quick & easy...even the fussiest kids love it when you let them help!*

8-oz. tube refrigerated crescent
   rolls
2 T. butter, melted
3-oz. pkg. strawberry gelatin
   mix

15-oz. can sliced peaches,
   drained and cubed

Separate rolls into 8 triangles. Brush triangles with melted butter;
sprinkle with gelatin mix and top evenly with peaches. Roll up each
triangle into a crescent as directed on package. Arrange on a large
greased baking sheet. Bake at 350 degrees for 12 to 15 minutes, or
until golden. Let cool slightly before serving. Makes 8 servings.

Use a sugar shaker to save clean-up time in the kitchen...
it's ideal for dusting powdered sugar onto cookies and
desserts warm from the oven.

Desserts IN A JIFFY

Apple Crisp Pizza

Jackie Balla
Walbridge, OH

As soon as farmstands open in the fall, we stop for apples to make this new twist on an old stand-by dessert. Try it with pears too!

13.8-oz. tube refrigerated pizza
   crust dough
2/3 c. sugar
3 T. all-purpose flour
1 t. cinnamon

4 Granny Smith apples,
   cored, peeled and cut into
   1/2-inch slices
1/2 c. caramel ice cream topping
Optional: vanilla ice cream

Spread dough on a greased 12" pizza pan. Combine sugar, flour and cinnamon in a bowl; add apples and toss. Arrange apples in a single layer to completely cover dough; sprinkle with Oat Topping. Bake at 350 degrees for 30 minutes. Remove from oven; immediately drizzle with caramel topping. Cut into wedges and serve warm, with scoops of ice cream if desired. Makes 15 to 18 servings.

Oat Topping:

1/2 c. all-purpose flour
1/3 c. brown sugar, packed
1/3 c. quick-cooking oats,
   uncooked

1 t. cinnamon
1/4 c. butter, softened

Toss dry ingredients to mix; blend in butter until crumbly.

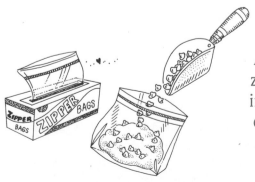

A time-saving tip! Fill plastic zipping bags with dry topping ingredients for a favorite fruit crisp or cobbler...just add the wet ingredients later.

Quick Chocolate Mousse

Geneva Rogers
Gillette, WY

*If you're a coffee lover, stir in some instant coffee granules
for a yummy mocha mousse.*

14-oz. can sweetened
   condensed milk
1 c. cold water
3.9-oz. pkg. instant chocolate
   pudding mix

8-oz. container frozen whipped
   topping, thawed and divided

Whisk together condensed milk and water in a large bowl. Add pudding mix; beat well. Chill 5 minutes. Fold in 2 cups whipped topping; chill until serving time. Garnish with dollops of remaining topping. Makes 8 to 10 servings.

Cupcakes for dessert tonight? Frost them quickly
by dipping in frosting, then toss on some chocolate chips
or colored sprinkles just for fun.

Desserts IN A JIFFY

Grandmother's Waffle Cookies

Shannon Sitko
Warren, OH

My grandmother, Blanche White, always made these delicious cookies...
she would even keep bags of them in the freezer for us. My Aunt Cheryl
gave me the recipe and now my own children love them as much as I do.

1 c. butter, melted and slightly
   cooled
4 eggs, beaten
1 c. sugar
1 c. brown sugar, packed

2 t. vanilla extract
4 c. all-purpose flour

Mix together melted butter, eggs and sugars; add vanilla. Slowly mix in flour. Drop teaspoonfuls of batter onto a preheated ungreased waffle iron. Check cookies after about one minute. Cookies are done when they are a medium golden in center and light golden at the edges. Makes 3 dozen.

Whirl up some iced cappuccino for an easy, refreshing dessert.
In a blender, combine a can of sweetened condensed milk,
2 cups cold water and a tablespoon of instant coffee granules.
Add a cup of ice cubes, cover and blend until smooth and frothy.
Pour into tall glasses...yum!

Serendipity Squares

Carrie Fostor
Baltic, OH

Need a potluck goodie in a hurry? Try this quick recipe!

18-1/2 oz. pkg. yellow cake mix
2 eggs, beaten
1/2 c. oil
2 T. water

12-oz. pkg. semi-sweet
   chocolate chips
3 c. mini marshmallows

Mix all ingredients together in a large bowl. Pour mixture evenly into a greased and floured 13"x9" baking pan. Bake at 350 degrees for 20 to 25 minutes. Cut into squares. Makes one dozen.

Angel Bars

Paula Spadaccini
Shelburne, VT

A sweet old-fashioned treat, made with just 4 ingredients.

16-oz. pkg. angel food cake mix
22-oz. can lemon pie filling
1 c. sweetened flaked coconut or
   chopped walnuts

Garnish: powdered sugar

In a large bowl, mix together all ingredients except powdered sugar. Spread in a 13"x9" baking pan that has been greased on the bottom only. Bake at 350 degrees for 25 to 30 minutes. Sift powdered sugar over top while still warm; cut into squares. Makes 16 servings.

Desserts IN A JIFFY

Creamy Pineapple Dessert

Lisa Johnson
Hallsville, TX

My sister, Lori, shared this recipe with me...it came with the funny but descriptive name of "4 Tins and a Tub!" Yum!

20-oz. can crushed pineapple, drained
20-oz. can pineapple chunks, drained
14-oz. can sweetened condensed milk

22-oz. can lemon pie filling
8-oz. container frozen whipped topping, thawed

Mix all ingredients in a large bowl. Keep chilled until serving time. Serve cold. Makes 8 to 10 servings.

Give pastries a special touch with a drizzle of white chocolate! Fill a small plastic zipping bag with white chocolate chips and microwave briefly until melted. Snip off a tiny corner and squeeze to drizzle, then toss away the empty bag.

Kim's Peach Cobbler

Beth Smith
Manchester, MI

*When I was first married, a co-worker shared this easy dessert with me.
She has since moved on, but I will always remember her every time
I make this cobbler. Share a recipe and be remembered forever!*

1 c. sugar
1 egg, beaten
1 t. vanilla extract
1 c. all-purpose flour

15-oz. can sliced peaches,
 drained
1/2 c. butter, melted

Stir sugar, egg and vanilla until well blended; mix in flour. Place
peaches in the bottom of a lightly greased 9"x9" baking pan. Pour
batter over peaches; drizzle with melted butter. Bake at 350 degrees
for 20 to 40 minutes, or until light golden and crunchy on top.
Serves 6.

Pat a tube of refrigerated cookie dough into an ungreased
13"x9" baking pan. Bake at 350 degrees for 12 to 18 minutes.
Let cool slightly before cutting into bars...so much quicker
than making drop cookies!

Desserts IN A JIFFY

Mom's Pistachio Dessert

Autumn Bock
Fife, WA

This is a yummy make-ahead dessert. I always looked forward to this dessert when my mom made it...now I make it, and my husband raves about how good it is!

1 c. all-purpose flour
1/2 c. margarine, softened
1/2 c. chopped walnuts
8-oz. pkg. cream cheese,
   softened
1 c. powdered sugar

8-oz. container frozen whipped
   topping, thawed and divided
2 3.4-oz. pkgs. pistachio
   pudding mix
3 c. milk
1/2 c. slivered almonds

Combine flour, margarine and walnuts; mix well and spread in an greased 13"x9" baking pan. Bake at 325 degrees for 15 minutes; let cool. Combine cream cheese, powdered sugar and one cup whipped topping; blend well and spread on top of cooled crust. Combine pudding mixes and milk. Mix as package directs; spread pudding over cream cheese layer. Frost with remaining whipped topping; sprinkle with almonds. Chill until serving time. Makes 12 servings.

Make a luscious sauce for pound cake...simply purée fruit preserves with a few tablespoons of fruit juice.

Fresh Strawberry Fool

Lisa Ashton
Aston, PA

*Whip up this cool and elegant dessert for pop-in guests...
that's anything but foolish!*

1/2 c. whipping cream
1/3 c. powdered sugar
1/2 t. vanilla extract
8-oz. container lemon yogurt

3 c. strawberries, hulled and
   sliced
1/2 c. shortbread cookies,
   coarsely crumbled

With an electric mixer on high speed, beat whipping cream, powdered
sugar and vanilla until soft peaks form. Fold in yogurt with a spoon.
Spoon mixture into 8 parfait glasses. Layer with sliced berries and
sprinkle with crumbled cookies. Serve immediately or keep chilled
until serving time. Makes 8 servings.

Do-it-yourself sandwich cookies for kids...pick up
a box of graham crackers and a container of frosting.
Give 'em a spatula and just turn 'em loose!

Desserts IN A JIFFY

Easy Apple Popovers

Debra Coogle
Oglethorpe, GA

These fruity treats are delish and oh-so easy! I made up this recipe one day when I needed a dessert to carry to the family of a friend who had just come home from the hospital.

10-oz. tube refrigerated
    flaky biscuits
2 c. sweetened applesauce

1 c. powdered sugar
3 to 4 T. milk

Spray a muffin tin with non-stick vegetable spray. Separate biscuits. Press a biscuit into the bottom and partway up the sides of each muffin cup. Spoon applesauce into biscuits. Bake at 300 degrees for about 10 to 15 minutes, until biscuits are done. Remove popovers from muffin tin; let cool. Mix powdered sugar and milk to a drizzling consistency; drizzle over popovers. Makes 10 servings.

Create a heavenly glaze for any apple dessert. Melt together
1/2 cup butterscotch chips, 2 tablespoons butter and
2 tablespoons whipping cream over low heat.

Harvest Pumpkin Mousse

Annette Ingram
Grand Rapids, MI

Sprinkle with a crunchy topping of crushed gingersnap cookies.

1-oz. pkg. sugar-free instant
   butterscotch pudding mix
1-1/2 c. milk
1/2 c. canned pumpkin

1 t. pumpkin pie spice
1 c. frozen whipped topping,
   thawed and divided

Whisk together pudding mix and milk for 2 minutes; let stand for
2 minutes, until softly set. Fold in pumpkin, spice and 1/2 cup
whipped topping. Spoon into 4 dessert bowls; chill until serving time.
Dollop with remaining whipped topping. Serves 4.

Turn a bakery fruit pie into an extra-special dessert. (Shh....it's
your little secret!) Warm pie in the oven, then layer spoonfuls
of pie in parfait glasses with creamy whipped topping.
Garnish with chopped nuts or a dusting of cinnamon.

Desserts IN A JIFFY

Hot Fudge Ice Cream Cake

Linda Nowak
Cheektowaga, NY

A delectable make-ahead dessert that takes only minutes to assemble.

16 ice cream sandwiches
16-oz. container frozen whipped
   topping, thawed

2 12-oz. jars hot fudge topping
1/2 c. Spanish peanuts

Arrange 8 ice cream sandwiches in a single layer in a 13"x9" baking pan. Spread with one-half of whipped topping; add one-third of fudge topping and one-half of nuts. Layer with remaining sandwiches, remaining topping, one-third of fudge topping and remaining nuts; drizzle with remaining fudge topping. Freeze until firm, about 3 hours. Cut into squares to serve. Serves 16.

Butterscotch Sauce

Vickie

Dress up slices of store-bought cake or scoops of ice cream with a dollop of this tempting homemade sauce.

1/2 c. brown sugar, packed
1/2 c. whipping cream

2 T. butter, sliced

Combine ingredients in a small heavy saucepan. Cook over medium heat, stirring occasionally, until brown sugar dissolves and sauce thickens, about 5 minutes. Cool slightly before serving. Keep refrigerated. Makes 3/4 cup.

Instant ice cream social! Alongside pints of favorite ice cream flavors, set out toppings like sliced bananas, peanuts, maraschino cherries, hot fudge and whipped cream. Don't forget the jimmies!

Cherry Dump Dessert

Tamara Long
Huntsville, AR

My mom first tried this tasty recipe one day when she needed a quick dessert for a church supper. It soon became a family favorite and a potluck standard.

20-oz. can cherry pie filling
8-oz. container sour cream
8-oz. container frozen whipped
    topping, thawed

16-oz. pkg. chocolate chip
    cookies, divided

Stir together pie filling, sour cream and whipped topping in a large serving bowl. Crumble all except 6 cookies; gently fold crumbs into mixture. Arrange reserved cookies on top; chill until ready to serve. Makes 6 to 8 servings.

What's better than a pink lemonade pie? Two pies...one to enjoy, one to share! Thaw a small can of frozen pink lemonade concentrate and a small container of frozen whipped topping. Mix lemonade with a can of sweetened condensed milk, fold in whipped topping and spread into two graham cracker crusts. Refrigerate pies until firm.

Desserts IN A JIFFY

Peach & Blueberry Cobbler

Amanda Clark
Bristol, TN

*My friends are always impressed when I serve this dessert...there are
never any leftovers! If you want to double the recipe, use a
13"x9" baking pan and bake for 30 to 40 minutes.*

15-oz. can sliced peaches,
   drained
17.8-oz. pkg. blueberry quick
   bread mix with canned
   blueberries

cinnamon to taste
1/2 c. butter, melted
Garnish: vanilla ice cream

Spread peaches in the bottom of an ungreased 8"x8" baking pan.
Drain blueberries and spread over peaches; sprinkle with cinnamon.
Add quick bread mix to melted butter; stir together. Allow mixture
to cool slightly; crumble evenly over blueberries. Sprinkle with
cinnamon. Bake at 350 degrees for 20 to 30 minutes, or until golden.
Serve warm with ice cream. Serves 4.

Enjoy fresh-baked cookies at a moment's notice. Roll your
favorite cookie dough into balls and freeze them on a tray,
then pop them into a freezer bag. Later, just pull out the number
of cookies you need, thaw briefly and bake.

Peanut Butter Criss-Cross Cookies
Brenda Mulliniks
Henryetta, OK

*My youngest son, Eric, loves these scrumptious cookies so much
that he learned to bake them himself!*

1 egg, beaten
1 c. sugar
1 c. brown sugar, packed
1 c. shortening
1 t. vanilla extract

1 c. creamy or crunchy peanut
   butter
2 t. baking soda
1/2 t. salt
2 c. all-purpose flour

Mix egg, sugars, shortening, vanilla and peanut butter in a large bowl;
stir until creamy. Sift remaining ingredients together and stir into peanut
butter mixture. Drop by teaspoonfuls onto ungreased baking sheets.
Flatten cookies with a fork in a criss-cross pattern. Bake at 350 degrees
for 10 minutes; cool on a wire rack. Makes about 2 dozen.

"Fried" ice cream is a fun & festive ending to a Mexican meal.
Roll scoops of ice cream in a mixture of crushed frosted
corn flake cereal and cinnamon. Garnish with a drizzle of
honey and a dollop of whipped topping. They'll ask for seconds!

Desserts IN A JIFFY

Oatmeal Scotchies

Laurelle Heimbaugh
Gilbert, IA

This is an old, old recipe! I am so glad to be able to share it with others so they can enjoy it too.

2 c. all-purpose flour
2 t. baking powder
1 t. baking soda
1 t. salt
1 c. butter, softened

1-1/2 c. brown sugar, packed
2 eggs, beaten
1-1/2 c. long-cooking oats, uncooked
12-oz. pkg. butterscotch chips

In a small bowl, combine flour, baking powder, baking soda and salt; set aside. In a large bowl, combine butter, brown sugar and eggs; beat until creamy. Gradually add flour mixture; stir in oats and butterscotch chips. Drop by rounded tablespoonfuls onto ungreased baking sheets. Bake at 375 degrees for 10 minutes. Makes 4 dozen.

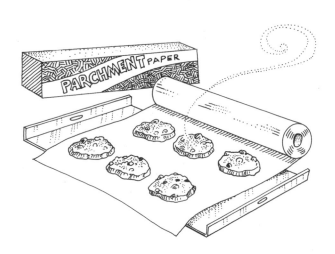

Cookies won't stick to baking sheets lined with parchment paper. Clean-up is a snap too...just toss away the paper.

Berry Patch Tarts

Marlene Burns
Swisher, IA

Very easy for kids to do...they'll be so proud of their creation!

8-oz. container mixed berry
   yogurt
2 c. frozen whipped topping,
   thawed

6 mini graham cracker crusts
Garnish: blueberries, raspberries

Stir yogurt and whipped topping together. Spoon into tart crusts; cover and freeze for 20 minutes. Top with berries. Serves 6.

Orange Cloud Dessert

Julie Brown
Malvern, OH

Stir up this cool, fruity dessert in a jiffy.

2 c. water
3-oz. pkg. orange gelatin mix
3.4-oz. pkg. instant vanilla
   pudding mix

8-oz. container frozen whipped
   topping, thawed
11-oz. can mandarin oranges,
   drained

In a medium saucepan, bring water to a boil over medium heat. Add gelatin and pudding mixes; whisk and boil for 2 minutes. Chill in saucepan just until set; fold in whipped topping and oranges. Transfer to a serving bowl; chill until ready to serve. Makes 8 servings.

Need a quick snack for the kids? Make fruit pops! Blend together fresh or canned fruit with fruit juice and pour into ice cube trays or small paper cups. Insert wooden sticks before freezing.

Desserts **IN A JIFFY**

Banana Supreme Pie

Regina Kostyu
Gooseberry Patch

Shh...don't tell anyone how easy this is to make!

3.4-oz. pkg. instant vanilla
    pudding mix
1 c. sour cream
1/2 c. milk

12-oz. container frozen whipped
    topping, thawed
1 to 2 ripe bananas, sliced
9-inch graham cracker crust

Stir together pudding mix, sour cream, milk and whipped topping; set aside. Arrange banana slices in bottom of pie crust. Spoon pudding mixture over bananas; chill until serving time. Makes 6 servings.

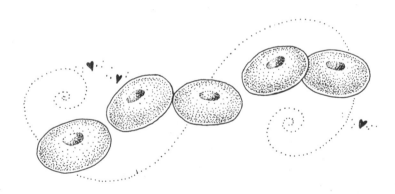

Doughnuts in a dash! Separate refrigerated biscuits and cut out a hole in the center of each. Fry biscuits in hot oil until golden on both sides; drain on paper towels. Roll in sugar and serve warm.

Millionaire Brownies

Mary Nguyen
Oklahoma City, OK

These are the very best brownies I had ever had...they're a big hit with my family too!

18-1/4 oz. pkg. chocolate fudge cake mix
1 c. evaporated milk, divided
3/4 c. butter, softened
14-oz. pkg. caramels, unwrapped

1-1/2 c. semi-sweet chocolate chips
1-1/2 c. chopped pecans

Stir dry cake mix, 2/3 cup evaporated milk and butter until moistened. Spread half the mixture in the bottom of a greased 13"x9" baking pan. Bake at 350 degrees for 8 minutes; cool. Heat caramels and remaining evaporated milk in a small saucepan over low heat, stirring constantly, until caramels are melted. Sprinkle brownies with chocolate chips; drizzle with caramel mixture. Top with pecans. Spread remaining batter over top. Bake at 350 degrees for 18 to 20 minutes. Cool completely before cutting. Makes 2 dozen.

My advice to you is not to inquire why or whither, but just enjoy your ice cream while it is on your plate.
-Thornton Wilder

Desserts IN A JIFFY

Choco-Berry Cookie Drops

Edward Smulski
Lyons, IL

Two kinds of chocolate chips plus tangy raspberry jam...delightful!

18-1/4 oz. pkg. devil's food
   cake mix
1/2 c. oil
2 eggs, beaten
1/2 c. white chocolate chips

1/2 c. semi-sweet chocolate
   chips
1/2 t. vanilla extract
1/2 c. raspberry jam

Blend dry cake mix, oil and eggs together until well mixed. Add chocolate chips, vanilla and jam; blend well. Drop by well-rounded teaspoonfuls onto lightly greased baking sheets, leaving room for cookies to expand. Bake at 350 degrees for 12 minutes. Makes 3 to 4 dozen.

Serve brownie sundaes for an extra-special treat! Place brownies on individual dessert plates and top with a scoop of ice cream and a drizzle of chocolate syrup. Irresistible!

Super-Good Peachy Cake

Veronnica Watson
San Jose, CA

In a word...yum!

16-oz. container cottage cheese
2 3-oz. pkgs. peach gelatin mix
8-oz. can crushed pineapple,
 drained
16-oz. pkg. frozen peaches,
 thawed and divided

16-oz. baked angel food cake
16-oz. container frozen whipped
 topping, thawed

In a medium bowl, mix together cottage cheese, gelatin mix, pineapple and two-thirds of the peaches. Set aside. Place cake on a cake plate. Frost cake with whipped topping, making sure all sides are evenly covered. Spoon cottage cheese mixture over top and down center of cake. Arrange remaining peaches on top of cake. Any remaining fruit mixture can be spooned over individual slices of cake. Serve immediately. Makes 8 to 10 servings.

Fruit kabobs are a sweet ending to any meal. Arrange chunks of pineapple and banana, plump strawberries and kiwi slices on skewers. For a creamy dipping sauce, blend together 1/2 cup each of cream cheese and marshmallow creme.

Desserts IN A JIFFY

Strawberry Angel Cake

Lisa Johnson
Hallsville, TX

*Your family & friends will think you're an angel
when you serve this cake.*

16-oz. baked angel food cake
2 c. whipping cream
2/3 c. strawberry ice cream
   topping

2 pts. strawberries, hulled and
   halved

Slice cake horizontally into 4 layers; set aside. In a chilled bowl with an electric mixer on high speed, beat whipping cream and topping until stiff peaks form. Place bottom layer of cake on a cake plate; frost with a 1/2-inch layer of whipped cream mixture. Repeat with remaining layers. Frost entire cake with remaining whipped cream mixture, making sure to cover top and sides of cake. Arrange berries over top and sides, pressing firmly into whipped cream. Serve immediately or keep chilled up to 8 hours. Makes 10 servings.

Festive cupcakes...just the thing for tomorrow's bake sale!
Stir up a cake mix and fill bright-colored paper liners
2/3 full. Top batter with 2 teaspoons mini candy-coated
chocolates per cupcake. Press toppings lightly into
batter and bake as usual. No frosting needed!

Chocolate Chip Spice Bars

Carla Myhre-Vogt
Buffalo, MN

When I first tried this recipe, the bars were speedy to make,
but pretty bland. I decided to try adding the spice mix
from another bar recipe...that did the trick!

18-1/4 oz. pkg. yellow cake mix
1/2 c. oil
2 eggs, beaten
2 t. cinnamon
1/2 t. nutmeg
1/2 t. ground cloves
1 c. semi-sweet chocolate chips

Blend together dry cake mix, oil, eggs and spices. Press into an ungreased 13"x9" baking pan; sprinkle chocolate chips over top. Bake at 350 degrees for 10 to 15 minutes, or just until golden. Cool and cut into bars. Makes about 2-1/2 dozen.

Rah-Rah Buckeye Bars

Marsha Porter
Marysville, OH

The same irresistible flavor as our favorite buckeye candies,
but so much easier to fix!

1 c. creamy peanut butter
1 c. butter
2 c. graham cracker crumbs
10-oz. pkg. milk chocolate chips
6 T. oil

Combine peanut butter and butter in a microwave-safe dish. Microwave on high setting until softened. Stir in graham cracker crumbs; mix well. Pat into a lightly greased 13"x9" baking pan; set aside. Melt chocolate chips in a saucepan over low heat; stir in oil. Pour over peanut butter base; place in refrigerator to cool. Cut into small bars after 30 minutes, while bars are still slightly soft. Makes 3 to 4 dozen.

Desserts IN A JIFFY

Best-Ever Mud Pie

Cheryl Lagler
Zionsville, PA

This decadent dessert is put together in no time...it will be eaten up even quicker, I guarantee!

1 c. sugar
2 eggs, beaten
1/2 c. margarine, melted and cooled slightly
1 t. vanilla extract
1/3 c. all-purpose flour
1/3 c. baking cocoa
1/4 t. salt

Optional: 1 c. chopped pecans or walnuts
1/4 c. hot fudge ice cream topping
8-oz. container frozen whipped topping, thawed
Optional: vanilla or coffee ice cream

Combine sugar, eggs, margarine, vanilla, flour, cocoa and salt; mix well. Stir in nuts, if using; pour into a greased 9" pie plate. Bake at 325 degrees for 25 minutes. Remove from oven; immediately poke holes in the top with a toothpick. Spread fudge topping over pie; cool completely. Keep refrigerated. At serving time, spread whipped topping over pie. Serve with scoops of ice cream, if desired. Makes 6 to 8 servings.

Everybody loves s'mores! Here's a new way to make them. Sprinkle chocolate chips and mini marshmallows on a flour tortilla. Roll up and microwave for 5 to 15 seconds, until warm and melted. Enjoy right away...mmm!

Whether you make a whole meal or add a home-cooked touch to take-out food or freezer favorites, there are

Fast-Fix MEALS
for any occasion!

Here are just a few menu suggestions to show how easy menu planning can be with our fast-fix recipes!

A BUSY-DAY PANTRY MEAL

Speedy Chicken Spaghetti, p. 70
Tossed salad with Italian salad dressing
Cheesy Garlic Bread, p. 188
Garlicky Spinach, p. 142
Grandmother's Waffle Cookies, p. 197

A FESTIVE FAMILY DINNER

Tuscan Dipping Oil, p. 174
   with French bread
Tomato & Spinach Soup, p. 102
Easy Garlic-Parmesan Chicken, p. 91
Parsley Baked Rice, p. 143
Toasty Green Beans & Walnuts, p. 155
Harvest Pumpkin Mousse, p. 204

AN EASY GAME-DAY PARTY

Eric's Favorite Sauce, p. 192 *with fresh veggie dippers*

Mother's Pull-Apart Cheese Bread, p. 190

Brown Sugar Barbecues, p. 120

Pan-Fried Oven Potatoes, p. 165

Parmesan Zucchini Sticks, p. 159

Rah-Rah Buckeye Bars, p. 216

A LEISURELY BACKYARD PICNIC

Weekend Treat Burgers, p. 128

Simple Coleslaw, p. 172

Kristen's Baked Beans, p. 162

Tortilla chips with salsa

Banana Supreme Pie, p. 211

INDEX

Breads

Cheesy Garlic Bread, 188
Cinnamon-Apple Muffins, 177
Corn & Green Chile Muffins, 186
Diane's Skillet Cornbread, 173
French Onion Biscuits, 182
Mother's Pull-Apart Cheese Bread, 190
Pamm's Deluxe Garlic Bread, 168
Sharon's Banana Muffins, 176
Sweet Potato Cornbread, 178

Desserts

Angel Bars, 198
Apple Crisp Pizza, 195
Banana Supreme Pie, 211
Berry Patch Tarts, 210
Berry Peachy Twists, 194
Best-Ever Mud Pie, 217
Butterscotch Sauce, 205
Cherry Dump Dessert, 206
Choco-Berry Cookie Drops, 213
Chocolate Chip Spice Bars, 216
Creamy Pineapple Dessert, 199
Easy Apple Popovers, 203
Fresh Strawberry Fool, 202
Grandmother's Waffle Cookies, 197
Harvest Pumpkin Mousse, 204
Hot Fudge Ice Cream Cake, 205
Kim's Peach Cobbler, 200
Millionaire Brownies, 212
Mom's Pistachio Dessert, 201
Oatmeal Scotchies, 209
Orange Cloud Dessert, 210
Peach & Blueberry Cobbler, 207
Peanut Butter Criss-Cross Cookies, 208
Quick Chocolate Mousse, 196
Rah-Rah Buckeye Bars, 216
Serendipity Squares, 198
Strawberry Angel Cake, 215
Super-Good Peachy Cake, 214

Mains-Beef

Becky's Ground Beef Casserole, 79
Beef & Rice Hot Pot, 51
Beef Skillet Fiesta, 7
Cabbage Crescent Rolls, 87
Cheesy Beefy Squash Casserole, 93
Connie's Skillet Meatloaf, 60
Cowpoke Casserole, 67
Favorite Hamburger Goulash, 39
Grandma's Hot Dog Skillet Meal, 33
Ground Beef & Noodles, 30
Ground Beef Stroganoff, 61
Hearty Shepherd's Pie, 66
Hodge Podge, 42
Husband-Pleasin' Dirty Rice, 32
Jax's Cheeseburger Pizza, 77
Katie's Taco Casserole, 84
Layered Mexican Pizzas, 78
Loaded Potato Casserole, 82
Lomo Saltado, 20
Mary's Meatballs, 86
Roma Burgers on Spaghetti, 44
Skillet Surprise, 19
Sloppy Joe Casserole, 76
Speedy Burritos, 85
Speedy Goulash, 11
Teeny's Mexican Casserole, 71
Zucchini & Beef in Wine Sauce, 62

Mains-Chicken & Turkey

Balsamic Chicken & Rice, 40
Basil Chicken Skillet, 64
Cheesy Chicken-Tomato Pasta, 17
Chicken Alfredo Florentine, 54
Chicken Fajitas, 6
Chicken in the Garden, 63
Chicken Oregano, 80
Chicken Pizza Pizazz, 94
Chicken Pot Pie, 68
Chicken Presto, 56

INDEX

Chicken Turnovers, 69
Chicken-Broccoli Stir-Fry, 34
Creamed Chicken on Toast, 28
Easy Garlic-Parmesan Chicken, 91
Easy Turkey Noodle Bake, 92
Honey Chicken & Stuffing, 90
Honey Chicken Stir-Fry, 8
Italian Chicken Spaghetti, 49
Kimberly's Taquito Bake, 88
Lemony Skillet Chicken, 16
Mexican Chicken Olé, 57
Mushroom-Garlic Chicken Pizza, 81
Salsa Chicken, 70
Speedy Chicken Spaghetti, 70
Speedy Skillet Lasagna, 38
Stuffed Chicken Breasts, 36
Sweet-and-Sour Popcorn Chicken, 22
Yummy Corn Quesadillas, 13
Zesty Ranch Chicken, 80

Mains-Fish & Seafood

Creamy Shrimp Stir-Fry, 24
Salmon Delight, 75
Shrimp & Tomato Italiano, 14
Stovetop Tuna Casserole, 25
Twistin' Tilapia, 74

Mains-Meatless & Veggie

Broccoli con Fettuccine, 15
Cheesy Corn & Bean Burritos, 89
Chili Rellenos Casserole, 73
Grandma Goldie's Sketti, 31
Jill's Spicy Tomato Pasta, 48
Macaroni & Cheese Deluxe, 83
Moira's Marinara Sauce, 58
Nutty Rice & Spinach Toss, 29
Skillet Macaroni & Cheese, 52
Vickie's Enchilada Bake, 72

Mains-Pork

Antipasto-Style Linguine, 59
Apricot-Glazed Pork Chops, 21
Cheddar Spaghetti, 55
Country Pork Chop Dinner, 50
Easy Pork Chops & Rice, 18
French Bread Sausage Pizza, 94
Golden Breaded Pork Chops, 37
Italian Sausage Salad, 45
One-Pot Sausage Etouffee, 47
Potato & Ham Frittata, 26
Rustic Kielbasa Skillet, 9
Sausage & Pepper Bake, 46
Scrambled Mac & Cheese, 27
Shellye's Pizzadillas, 12
Simple Tater Supper, 10
Spicy Pork Noodle Bowls, 23
Stacey's Not Soup, 43
Zesty Penne & Peppers, 53

Salads & Dressings

Amy's Sweet & Super Dressing, 180
Apple Orchard Salad, 181
Blue Cheese Dressing, 185
Broccoli-Cashew Slaw, 179
Eric's Favorite Sauce, 192
Homemade Ranch Dressing, 183
Hula Salad, 171
Lemony Caesar Dressing, 174
Mom's Tomato Thing, 191
Moose's Garden Salad, 169
Raspberry Vinaigrette, 170
Red, Green & White Salad, 184
Ruby's 3-Bean Salad, 187
Simply Coleslaw, 172
Strawberry Vinaigrette, 170
Thousand Island Dressing, 185
Tomato Delight Dressing, 189
Tomato-Basil Salad, 175
Tuscan Dipping Oil, 174

INDEX

Sandwiches

Alberta Prairie Burgers, 123
Billie's Sloppy Joes, 131
Black Bean Burgers, 127
BLT Quesadilla, 121
BLT Tuna Sandwiches, 135
Brown Sugar Barbecues, 120
Chet's Bunsteads, 119
Cobb Salad Subs, 125
Corned Beef Bar-B-Cues, 120
Dagwood Burgers, 118
Excellent Burgers, 129
Greek Chicken Wraps, 133
Grilled Ham Panini, 138
Island Burgers, 136
Marty's Special Burgers, 124
Mom's Eggplant Sandwich, 126
Mom's Pizza Loaf, 130
Ranch Chicken Wraps, 132
Seaside Salmon Buns, 134
Turkey Gobbler Sandwich, 122
Weekend Treat Burgers, 128
Western Burgers, 137

Sides

Aunt Marcie's Fried Rice, 152
Colorful Rice Toss, 163
Country Beans & Potatoes, 162
Creamy Italian Noodles, 166
Crispy Baked Eggplant, 158
Foolproof Rice Pilaf, 154
Fried Apples & Onions, 144
Garlicky Spinach, 142
German Potato Pancakes, 161
Italian Green Beans, 142
Kristen's Baked Beans, 162
Lemony Linguine, 156
Mom's Corn Oysters, 150
Orzo Garden Medley, 157
Pan-Fried Oven Potatoes, 165

Parmesan Zucchini Sticks, 159
Parsley Baked Rice, 143
Peppers & Pierogies, 148
Quick Oniony Potatoes, 165
Rosemary & Garlic Potato Hash, 140
Saucy Zucchini & Tomatoes, 164
Speedy Baked Beans, 146
Spicy Braised Greens, 153
Super-Fast Scalloped Potatoes, 147
Susan's Shells & Potatoes, 141
Sweet & Nutty Couscous, 160
Sweet Yammies, 145
Teriyaki Beans & Sprouts, 153
Toasty Green Beans & Walnuts, 155
Tomato-Basil Linguine, 149
Weda's Stuffed Tomatoes, 151

Soups & Stews

A-to-Z Soup, 114
Aunt Joan's Broccoli-Cheese Soup, 113
BBQ Sloppy Joe Soup, 98
Cheesy Chicken Chowder, 110
Chris's Vegetable Beef Soup, 107
Dad's Chicken Stew, 106
Easy Cabbage Stew, 108
Easy Potato-Cheddar Soup, 111
Fishermen's Stew, 100
Golden Cream Soup, 109
Hearty Veggie Soup, 103
Italian Sausage Soup, 96
Lisa's Chicken Tortilla Soup, 105
Mexican Corn Soup, 104
Nana's Country Chili, 99
Oriental Broth with 3 Meats, 116
Savory Chicken Stew, 41
Simple Seafood Chowder, 101
Speedy Chicken Noodle Soup, 115
Speedy Meatball Soup, 97
Tomato & Spinach Soup, 102
Tortellini-Spinach Soup, 112